HIS PICTURE
IN
THE PAPERS

HIS PICTURE
IN
THE PAPERS

A Speculation
on Celebrity in America
Based on
the Life of Douglas Fairbanks, Sr.

By Richard Schickel

Charterhouse New York

For John and Dorothy Whedon, Gratefully

"Somewhere in the back of his head he may feel a little guilty about it . . . he resents people giving him attention, yet he also uses the attention to get power. I mean it's really an American trip. Very interesting. . . . They kick the photographers yet they want the attention. . . . That's it. To be a movie star."

—Jon Voight

"This celebrity business is quite chronic."

—Virginia Woolf

I

To see him at work—even now, over thirty years after his premature death, a half-century, more or less, since he made his finest films—is to sense, as if for the first time, the full possibilities of a certain kind of movement in the movies. The stunts have been imitated and parodied, and so has the screen personality, which was an improbable combination of the laughing cavalier and the dashing democrat. But no one has quite recaptured the freshness, the sense of perpetually innocent, perpetually adolescent narcissism, that Douglas Fairbanks brought to the screen. There was, of course, an element of the show-off in what he did, but it was (and still remains) deliciously palatable because he managed to communicate a feeling that he was as amazed and delighted as his audience by what that miraculous machine, his body, could accomplish when he launched it into the trajectory necessary to rescue the maiden fair, humiliate the villain, or escape the blundering soldiery that fruitlessly pursued him, in different uniforms but with consistent clumsiness, through at least a half-dozen pictures.

Watching him, indeed, one feels as one does watching an old comedy by Keaton or Chaplin: that somehow we have lost the knack, not to mention the spirit, for what they did, and that the loss is permanent. Undoubtedly there are people around to equal, even surpass, Fairbanks' athletic gift. But there is none, one sadly imagines, who could or would orchestrate those gifts as he did, creating out of a series of runs, jumps, leaps, vaults, climbs, swings, handsprings, somersaults, those miraculously long, marvelously melodic lines of movement through which he flung himself with such heedless grace. The problem is that even among the most youthful spirits in the acting game there is no disposition to see the aim of acting simply as taking joy from the job and giving it back—enhanced—to the audience. For actors, like everyone else these days, have grown distressingly sober about their missions in life. Fairbanks, on the other hand, was product and exemplar of an age that, if not quite so innocent as we like to suppose, was nevertheless not quite so grand in its artistic aspirations—especially in the movies, which only a few zealots could even imagine as an art form. There is absolutely no evidence that as an actor—or, to risk a pretentious term, an artist—Douglas Fairbanks conceived of himself as anything more than a fabulist and fantasist. And the idea that he might have held a mirror up to life would probably have appalled him. What he did was hold a mirror up to himself—to endlessly boyish Doug—and invite his audience to join him in pleased contemplation of the image he found there, an image that very accurately reflected the shallow, callow, charming man who lived by the simplest of American codes, and eventually died by it.

Let us, therefore, stipulate at the outset that his artistry—the one thing he was always too modest about—was a given factor in the equation of his personality. Of course, like all marvelous athletes, he submitted to the most rigorous discipline to keep in condition and to perfect those wonderous "stunts" (somehow the word seems too small to describe the miracles of motion he wrought). But the fact is that these, like his basic screen personality, were a natural outgrowth of his character—exaggerations, to be sure, of his natural ebullience and his need to express that ebullience physically, but nothing he had to force or study too hard.

Indeed, it is fair to say that, of the great stars of the silent screen—the ones who pioneered the genres and the characterological archetypes that for so long determined so much film content—Fairbanks probably expressed more of his true self on screen than anyone. Mary Pickford, with whom he was to contract Hollywood's first royal marriage, had created, of course, the classic American girl—spunky, virginal, with a beauty endlessly bathed in golden sunlight—but she was, in fact, a tough, shrewd woman and it would appear that her character began as a fantasy shared by her archetypal stage mother and her first film director, D. W. Griffith, and that it was sustained more by the demands of commerce than by the demands of artistic conscience. Chaplin's Little Fellow was a more complicated construct, and surely represented a part of his complex nature—but only a part of it. William S. Hart, the first great Western good-bad man, came in time to identify very strongly with his screen character, but his real-life Western experience was limited and, before the movies found him, he had been an actor in stage melodramas (notably *Ben Hur*) that had precious little to do with frontier days in the United States. As for vamps and other exotic sex symbols, from Theda Bara to Rudolph Valentino, they were all largely the products of the feverish imaginations of producers and publicists.

Fairbanks was, on the other hand, always—triumphantly, irritatingly, ingratiatingly—Fairbanks, both on the screen and away from it. Indeed, there is about his career a certain inevitability; one can't quite imagine what he would have done with himself if the movies had not come into existence and provided him with precisely the kind of showcase his spirit and his talents required. Many of his peers might have been just as successful (if not quite so wildly prosperous) as stage personalities. Others, rather ordinary souls beneath the exotic personas that were invented for them, might well have been far more comfortable in routine occupations, leading anonymous middle-class existences. But there was no stage—not even, finally, the movie stage—that could contain Fairbanks' energy or fully exploit his natural gifts. And he was, from earliest childhood, different from other children in ways that no one at the time could quite specify. From his personal history we gain a sense that none of the usual livelihoods would have satisfied him, that he had no choice but to carve his own, singular path in the world.

Indeed, it is perfectly clear that merely acting in films could never have been enough to contain his restless energy. Though that medium was more suited to him than the stage, he still needed more action, more excitement, a greater involvement in the creation of his films and in the management of his career and his image (to use a word not then in vogue) than had been possible for stage-bound actors, or than had at first seemed necessary in movies. The mass appeal of the movies, it must be remembered, had been established for only a little more than a decade, while the star system, the great organizing principle of the industry, was only in the experimental stage when he came to them.

What he had—in addition to his personal magnetism and his delightful energy—was the imagination to organize this organizing principle. How consciously he undertook the task it is impossible to say, but the fact was that, alone of the first generation of superstars (to use another word that came into common usage much later), he had one of those rare personalities that truly flourish best under the light of public attention. Miss Pickford appears to have tolerated it under a tight mask of queenly graciousness. It was part of the price she had to pay not just for economic security but for economic power. Chaplin and Hart were, each in his way, intensely private men. The former, preoccupied with the purification of his art and with the cultivation of respect among the handful of international figures he regarded as his artistic and intellectual peers, mostly shunned public display and, indeed, claimed that his only close friend was Fairbanks. Hart, too, was artistically preoccupied, intent on presenting to the public what he believed was an historically accurate representation of The American West—so much so that he retired from the screen abruptly, in revolt against what he regarded as vulgar commercial pressure to glamorize that history as it was presented on the screen. The other great silent stars who came to fame slightly after this group (Valentino was a notable example) were often either too weak or too unaware of what was happening to them to make more than confused and occasional stabs at the careful management of their public lives and images. They allowed others to handle these matters and quite often discovered too late that they had been wretchedly deceived, even unto the point of destruction. ("A man should control his life," Valentino once said. "Mine is controlling me. I don't like it.")

Fairbanks, however, was different. Only late in life, when his body betrayed him and he could no longer physically do what his spirit commanded, did he demonstrate discomfort over his highly public life and the demands it made of him. Until then he gave every evidence of relishing the attendant confusions of group creation (which any movie necessarily involves); was always, irrepressibly, the leader of that effort; and seemed to enjoy demonstrating mastery over his career almost as much as he enjoyed demonstrating mastery over his body. In short, in the entire history of the screen it is impossible to find anyone with a better temperament for, or a keener instinctual understanding of, what amounted to a new profession—that of being a movie star and a celebrity.

And let there be no mistake about that. This line of work *was* unprecedented. To be sure, there had been great, and greatly popular, stage stars in the United States throughout the nineteenth and early twentieth centuries. Their tours (and the tours of English and European artists capitalizing on their reputations in provincial America) had been major events in the cultural life of the nation. But their relationship to the public had been very different from the relationship movie stars would experience. For one thing, the stage is a less intimate medium (even though the audience is physically in the presence of the actors) because the proscenium has a profoundly distancing effect—no close-ups here. Moreover, the stars of the popular melodramatic and spectacular stage (whose audience was quickly taken over by movies) tended to submerge themselves in one or two or three roles (James O'Neil as the Count of Monte Cristo, for example, or William Gillette as Sherlock Holmes), and though they were much admired, they were able to keep their private lives and their public lives quite neatly separated. Indeed, there seems not to have been inordinate public interest in the former. Even the rise of a truly popular press, in the form of mass circulation dailies and large circulation national magazines, did not greatly impinge on their solitude. Content analyses of the major magazines up until 1920, for example, have indicated a singular preoccupation with political and business leaders and inventors and very little concern with show business figures, although occasionally these individuals were subjects of public adulation very like that visited on movie stars later. (In his excellent study *The Hero in America*, the late Dixon Wecter reprinted a sample of the mail William Jennings Bryan received during and after his 1896 campaign for the Presidency, and it has the same grotesque and pathetic qualities that film-star fan mail would later exhibit.) Which is to say there was a hunger in the land for a more romantic popular hero (Bryan, as the handsome "boy orator," briefly filled the bill before lapsing into buffoonery), and it was this hunger that the movies, quite by accident, began the process of satisfying. It was a process that greatly expanded as more magazines (including those devoted exclusively to film personalities) were born, just as radio and, latterly, television provided new and ever-expanding means for image-making, or buffing.

In short, what Fairbanks and the entire first generation of stars had to do, besides play their roles, was to serve as transitional figures in an era of revolutionary change in the media, change that was both creator and creation of a similar revolution in mass sensibility. What happened in this period was that the public ceased to insist that there be an obvious correlation between achievement and fame. It was no longer absolutely necessary for its favorites to perform a real-life heroic act, to invent a boon for mankind, to create a mighty business enterprise (on the whole, and especially in America, achievement in the arts was not until recently of any great consequence in the fame game). Beginning with the rise of the star system in Hollywood it was possible to achieve "celebrity" through attainments in the realms of play—spectator sports, acting—and almost immediately thereafter it became possible to become *a* celebrity (a new coinage describing a new phenomenon) simply by becoming . . . a celebrity; that is, in

Daniel J. Boorstin's fine phrase, to be "known for your well-known-ness."

This is not to imply that there was anything fraudulent about the achievements of Fairbanks and the other pioneers of this particular industry. Far from it. Many of them were extraordinarily gifted individuals who had to overcome the problem of having absolutely no precedents to guide them in their work. It is suggested that something like a quantum change occurred in the quality of public life during the period, roughly from 1915 to 1925, and that the problem it presented people like Fairbanks was that of keeping one foot firmly planted on the ground of traditional American values and the expectations those values created among their publics while trying at the same time to make a giant step forward into the unknown, into celebrity country, if you will.

Moreover, once the star system—and the technologically expanded media system that fed upon and was fed by it—began to function in something like the modern manner in the 1920s, our definition of reality began to alter. It is not too much to say that we then had two realities to contend with. Daily life, of course, remained—that reality that we experienced personally, using all our senses. Then, however, there was this other reality, the one we apprehended through the media and through the employment of one or at most two senses intensively. The people who existed in this separate reality—the stars and celebrities—were as familiar to us, in some ways, as our friends and neighbors. In many respects we were—and are—more profoundly involved with their fates than we are with those of most of the people we know personally. They command enormous amounts of our psychic energy and attention. It is not too much to say that we have, in about a half-century's time, reached a point where most issues, whether political, intellectual, or moral in nature, do not have real status—that is, literally, the status of the real—until they have been taken up, dramatized, in the celebrity world.

Indeed, it is now essential that the politician, the man of ideas, and the nonperforming artist become performers so that they may become celebrities so that, in turn, they may exert genuine influence on the general public.* It is also true that, in recent years, the politics of confrontation, far from being a manifestation of a genuinely radical, revolutionary impulse, have been instead a form of theater, staged by amateur, if clever, actors creating parts for themselves as "leaders," "spokesmen," thus gaining the attention of the media and status as instant celebrities. It is their way of moving over from the realm of ordinary reality to that other reality, that surreality (the word literally means super-reality), which is peopled exclusively by the well known.

---

* *Among Richard M. Nixon's many claims to fame will be the fact that he was the first incumbent President subjected to the new discipline known as "Psychohistory," a form of biography in which the writer does not bother to cloak the deplorable jargon of psychoanalysis in literary language but, as the saying goes, "lets it all hang out." Bruce Mazlish's* In Search of Nixon *(Basic Books, 1972), while stylistically barbarous, is not without interest. It presents the thesis that Nixon, uncertain of quite who he is, takes his identity from whatever role he happens to be playing at any given moment. At this writing (September 1973), he has been playing President—publicly and repeatedly stressing the loneliness of the office, the discipline required by the decision-making process, the dignity of his station, which prevents him from devoting attention to "murky, small, unimportant, vicious little things" like Watergate. While Mazlish notes that we are all, to some degree, role players, he makes much of the fact that Nixon, alone among our Presidents, was a devoted worker in amateur theatricals as a youth and was also a debater of note—a form of intellectual role playing that implies an ability to argue any side of any issue* pour le sport. *On this single point—that late in the life of the celebrity game we have accorded the greatest victory in American electoral history to a man who fits the psychological profile of an actor more neatly than has any other major politician, Mazlish is powerfully persuasive. That Nixon's jerky, awkward movements, his vulgar theatricality (the bust of Honest Abe Lincoln as set decoration when he appears on television to make statements of questionable accuracy to the nation), his total insensitivity to language, show him to be a very bad actor only adds irony. It seems possible that we are now so far gone in the notion that all public figures must, perforce, be actors, that ineptness becomes a kind of earnest of sincerity; nobody that bad, that lacking in slickness, can be completely a crook. If he were really wicked he would be so smooth we would never know the depths of his evil. So much for home wisdom. Or can it be that Nixon is so clever that, at least until Watergate, he deliberately played the role badly? The mind boggles.*

The reason for this is simple: It is in this surreal world that all significant national questions are personified and thus dramatized. In time these dramas reach dénouement, and when they do the essential decisions facing the nation are made. Or more often, are left unresolved as some new group of personalities, representing some new problem, elbows aside the players (and issues) that previously commanded our fascinated, outraged attention. For the patience of the media is short, and the attention span of the great audience even shorter.

This is not to agree with the proposition that the medium is the message. It is, however, to suggest that the media are anything but neutral, reportorial entities or a simple transmission belt for ideas. And that qualification implies that, to a greater degree than we allow ourselves to suppose, the quality of celebrity "acting" while in view of the media is a large—perhaps the largest—factor in determining national goals.

The purpose of this essay, therefore, is manifold. To begin with, its human subject is intrinsically interesting, not merely because he was a gifted actor in the conventional sense, but also because he chose to embody certain traits common to the American character: optimism, for example; emphasis on youthfulness, not merely as a stage in life but as a value; belief in the business ethic, the success ethic, pluck and luck and self-confidence. Those characteristics are now rather quaint-seeming. But they were prime majority values when he came on the scene, and his instinctive understanding of his ability to symbolize them, to build a career on them, was an instinct that all celebrities must possess if they are to maintain their careers for any significant length of time. Moreover, he was present at the creation of this new surreality. Again, more from instinct than from design, he devised methods of surviving and prospering in this new mode of existence that are still models for his successors and repay study, if only because that reality was a little simpler in his time, a little easier to understand than it is now. Finally, in his life drama as he improvised it, we can discern the archetypal celebrity drama, a rise and a fall that are now a part of our expectations when we confront each new public figure who seeks to command our attention by commanding the attention of the media.

II

This situation presents the conventional biographer with some interesting problems. It is part of the basic mythology of heroism in Western culture that the hero shall overcome great early obstacles before attaining godlike status. And, as we shall see, Douglas Fairbanks' childhood and youth were beset with modest, genuine difficulties. But looking back from the height of his achievement, he took pleasure in inventing, or at least greatly exaggerating, some of them. For example, he was to imply to at least one biographer that, at the beginning, there was fear in his family that he might turn out to be "exceptional" in the most dismal sense of the term, that is, retarded. And, according to his son Douglas, Jr., he liked in later life to tease his mother and his aunt on this point, enjoying the vehemence of their denial that they had ever, even fleetingly, entertained such a notion. His son believes this was a latter-day conceit of his father's puckish sensibility, though the possibility that it might have been a projection of a not uncommon childish anxiety cannot be entirely dismissed.

The anecdote, moreover, fits neatly with others to form a portrait of a more than usually troubled childhood, one which even without Fairbanks' exercise of autobiographical license would have served his mythic purposes. Still, understatement was never his forte. And it is apparently true that he was—considering the sunny adult he turned out to be—a fairly glum infant, rarely sending out those signals of contentment—smiles, cooings, gurglings—that parents wait so anxiously to observe. His principal pleasure, observable apparently even in the crawling stage, was risk-taking. By the time he was three he had, according to his niece, who (with a journalist's assistance) wrote a discreet but very useful biography, "climbed everything in the yard and had swung from every limb and rail." Indeed, on his third birthday his mother, overseeing the preparation of the celebratory cake, was interrupted by Robert Fairbanks, Douglas' senior by a year, crying, "Mamma, he's on the roof again." And sure enough, there he was, on top of the barn, having climbed a trellis to achieve his precarious perch. What bothered Mrs. Fairbanks more than the physical danger was his owlish expression. There was not a flicker of defiance or excitement in his dark, solemn countenance. She ordered him down and watched him flip casually over the eaves, find his footing on the latticework, and scramble down. When she spanked him his cries were perfunctory and so was his response to the lecture from his father that somewhat marred the family party that evening. The first time anyone could remember him smiling was when he attempted to fly off the same roof, crashed, and, uninjured, began roaring at his own absurdity.

There was one other possible explanation for the somewhat

withdrawn nature Fairbanks exhibited in early childhood. That was his remarkably dark complexion. "I was the blackest baby you ever saw," he commented later. "I was so dark . . . my mother was ashamed of me. When all the neighbors came around to look at the new baby, Mother would say, 'Oh, I don't want to disturb him now—he's asleep and I'd rather not.' She just hated to show such a dark baby."

Again, his son thinks his father may have exaggerated the difference this made, pointing out that he had blue-gray eyes and dark brown rather than black hair. Indeed, it seems his complexion was not so dark as that of his elder brother. Still, he did tan easily and his handsome burnishing under the southern California sun would be very largely responsible for the tanning craze that has proved to be perhaps the most enduring fad of the 1920s. He would, in fact, come to enjoy "telling some people he had American Indian blood, others Italian or Spanish, or whatever amused him to say at the moment," as Douglas, Jr., would later recall.

The point here, of course, is not to establish with precision just how dark Douglas Fairbanks was, but to note that he apparently felt his complexion was a factor in setting him somewhat apart from his contemporaries and to observe that this, too, was converted by him, in the years of his fame—however jokingly—into yet another obstacle of sorts that he had overcome. To a degree that can only be guessed at, it must have contributed something to his sense of isolation not only from parental regard, but from the whole milieu of his childhood.

One always distrusts easy psychological explanations for the basic patterns of a man's behavior, but Fairbanks was essentially a simple man, and in his case a simple explanation will probably suffice. As a child he needed more love than he received; his best weapon in the fight for approval was his natural athletic talent, and since a glum athlete seems (or seemed in those more innocent days) a contradiction in terms, he developed a personal style that would suit his strongest skill. A modern critic, Alexander Walker, reversed a loathsome propaganda phrase to sum up Fairbanks' screen character, and it fits just as well the private character he began developing as a boy: "joy through strength." In other words, everything began and ended for Fairbanks with his zealously developed, jealously guarded physical skills and well-being. Almost all the other prominent features of his youthful character (which persisted into his forties essentially unchanged) were based on it—the bouncing, boundless optimism, the perpetually youthful manner, the lack of concern about the future, which a man in good health could always face and cope with, even his taste for practical jokes of a very physical kind.

What, if any, were the deeper wounds he tried to hide behind this mask, and for a long time seemed to have succeeded in doing? They were classic—an unhappy and domineering mother, a failed and finally absent father. Ella, his mother, had been raised the daughter of a prosperous Massachusetts family in a socially secure, carefully sheltered comfort that did not prepare her very well for the vicissitudes she was shortly to experience. She married one John Fairbanks, owner of a flourishing plantation near New Orleans. Shortly after she bore their only child, however, Fairbanks died of tuberculosis and she discovered that business partners had swindled him out of most of his fortune. Thereafter she remarried—this time to a heavy-drinking and rather abusive young Georgian named Edward Wilcox, and after giving him a son she sought a divorce from him. The attorney who obtained it for her was a Baptist minister's son (with, as it turned out, the breed's legendary capacity for broadcasting wild oats) and a sometime Union officer who had become a prominent New York lawyer and president of the United States Bar Association, a predecessor of the American Bar Association. He had represented Ella's first husband and it was to this attorney that she turned for assistance in the difficult matter of separating herself from Wilcox. He did the job—and fell in love with his client. He did not feel, however, that he could maintain his position in New York legal and social circles as the husband of a divorced woman and so, quite bravely (he was considerably older than his bride), he accepted a friend's invitation to join him in Denver, where they hoped to finance large-scale exploitation of the silver strikes that had been made near what a contemporary observer called "that great braggart city."

Alas, the fortune Charles Ulman sought there eluded him. Worse, the gently raised Ella hated the brown, parched land and the raw, booming city on which it stood. Moreover, she was afflicted with a heavy burden of guilt. A year after they arrived, and before Ulman could properly establish himself, their first child, Robert, arrived. A year later, on May 23, 1883, the boy they christened Douglas Elton Thomas Ulman, was born. There is no doubt that in time Ella came to love both of them in an excessive, even smothering sort of way. But for the moment, trying to maintain a prosperous front without adequate help, they were resented because they added to her feeling that she had been ill used by life and that under its pressure she had betrayed her best self. For one thing, she had been raised a Catholic and though her children were raised in the faith, she of course had been forced to abandon it when she divorced Wilcox. Then, too, her third husband was half or a quarter Jewish (there is some dispute on the matter) and though he was proud of the fact, it apparently reinforced her feeling that she had strayed too far from her background. Finally, Ulman, who had accepted John Fairbanks' namesake in his home, would not accept her child by her second husband, and Ella was forced to abandon him to the care of an aunt, rarely to see him again.

Her pain might have been eased had Ulman's mining ventures worked out, but despite the fact that the family passed several supervisory summers on the site of his most promising claim—an experience Ella loathed almost as much as her boys loved it—they came to naught. In 1888 Ulman took a position as a paid speaker for Benjamin Harrison, the Republican Presidential candidate, went back to New York, and returned only once to Denver on some mysterious business. Douglas encountered him on the street during that stay and persuaded him to come home and visit his wife (Ulman had apparently been drinking fairly heavily) for a painfully strained reunion. After that, Douglas rarely saw his father again, though when he began to work in the theater Ulman occasionally came around to his dressing room and embarrassedly asked for handouts, which were, of course, forthcoming. According to Douglas, Jr., his father "maintained a certain grudge" against Ulman for neglecting his family, a feeling that was by no means discouraged by the embittered Ella. Douglas, Jr., adds however: "He did have pride in [his father's] formerly successful career and a rueful pity for what had subsequently happened to him."

More important, he attributed his interest in the stage to his father, who had been an amateur Shakespearean scholar and was wont to recite from The Bard at the smallest excuse. In his New York days Ulman had numbered a good many prominent theatrical people among his excellent connections and was an intimate of Edwin Booth, whom he resembled sufficiently so that they were frequently mistaken for one another. This somewhat tenuous connection with the theater was to have a bearing on Fairbanks' career, but it seems likely he would have found his way onto some stage or other even without a parental example to guide him. He was a poor student and an inveterate and much-punished prankster who very much needed to be the center of attention. The reward for his transgressions was often the enforced memorization of some Shakespearean passage, and that work—along with the one part of the school week that he looked forward to, the Friday recitations— surely helped bend the twig. In any case, by the time he was in his teens, his neighbor Burns Mantle, later to become a well-known drama critic (and editor of the annual *Best Plays* volume), said, "he would recite you as fine and florid an Antony's speech to the Romans as you ever heard. With gestures, too."

By this time, his mother had been reduced to taking in boarders, and he would perform for them. He also organized a backyard theater one summer, having gathered a certain skill in dialects by imitating the street peddlers—Irish, Italian, Jewish— who hawked their wares from carts passing his home. He even got a bit part with a touring company, using one of the accents he had acquired to play an Italian newsboy in *On the Bowery*, which starred Steve Brodie and recounted, in a highly colored fashion, the events leading up to Brodie's celebrated—if very likely fraudulent—leap from the Brooklyn Bridge.

His mother was not altogether happy about Fairbanks' interest in the drama, but that was less worrisome to her than his rambunctious high spirits. The gloomy infant had turned into an irrepressible youth, and at school, visits to the principal's office were almost weekly occurrences. The exact nature of most of these transgressions is lost to history, but it is known that he and Robert once loosed a carton of grass snakes on a crowded trolley car, and that on another occasion, when he was serving as an altar boy, Douglas spiked the sacramental wine with vinegar. All the while, of course, he was busy turning the world into a gym, making of ordinary obstacles (steps and fences, for example) and ordinary heights (porch roofs, for instance) occasions for crowd-pleasing displays of a boy in graceful motion.

Ella was, in any sensible way, copeless during this period. Mostly she tried to turn the clock back. She divorced Ulman (for desertion) and resumed her first husband's name, which she induced her third husband's boys to adopt as well. She also saw to it that they were raised in the Catholic faith, from which she was barred by her divorces, and, for good measure, insisted that Douglas take the temperance pledge, which he kept until quite late in his life, unlike his church affiliation, which was lost as his mother's had been, through an early divorce.

Whether "Mrs. Fairbanks" achieved through these expedients a measure of contentment we do not know. It is clear, however, that she was never able to take and hold a firm line with the rambunctious Douglas. Basically overindulgent of him after his father departed, she did try sternness—two years of a military school she could ill afford—but that had no discernible effect on him. Thereafter, she enrolled him in drama school, no doubt thinking he might thus get acting out of his system before he was completely poisoned by it. (There are occasional mentions of a brief stay at a mining college in some accounts of his life, but they are unsubstantial and unsubstantiated.)

Alas, it was too late. His teacher, Margaret Fealy, was a retired actress of some repute, and she apparently sensed a genuine gift in the energetic young man, though she was never quite able to name what it was. At any rate, he confirmed his sense of vocation under her tutelage. He was seen in one of the productions in which Miss Fealy showcased her school's talent by Frederick Warde, a well-regarded actor-manager who had made most of his career on the road, and though he scarcely gave Fairbanks a rave—"that dark-haired youngster has more vigor than virtuosity"—the young optimist chose to interpret his comment as encouraging. Moreover, Warde had also been a friend of Booth's and had probably known Fairbanks' father as well during his New York days. But the sixteen-year-old's attempts to trade on this somewhat tenuous connection were repeatedly rebuffed at the stage door. Whereupon he resorted to his acrobatic skill, scaling the theater's outside wall to burst through the star's dressing-room window and gain an audience. Warde's surprise gave way to anger, which, in turn, gave way to amusement as the force of the youth's cheeky charm asserted itself. Warde gave him a job as an extra in crowd scenes—if he would agree to help clean the stage after each performance. He polished up the hardwood so faithfully that, as he prepared to depart, Warde promised him a job if Fairbanks could somehow find a way to quit school and join the company.

Leaving school turned out to be easy: on St. Patrick's Day he simply placed green hats and bows on all the busts of the famous men that lined the school's corridors, and he was expelled. Now came the hard part: talking Mom into letting him go into the theater. Here a friendly parish priest helped out, slyly suggesting that Douglas might have a religious vocation himself and could combine it with a suitably adventurous life by becoming a missionary in Africa. It was a ploy, but he was careful not to let Douglas in on it, lest conscious role-playing hinder the fine religious fervor the lad worked up. Ella, as the priest expected, decided that if acting lacked something in respectability it at least did not put her son in imminent peril of the cannibals' pot and so, partially financed by John Fairbanks, her first-born, who was a traveling salesman, she and Douglas set out to seek his fortune in New York. The year was 1900. Fairbanks was seventeen years old.

Warde kept his word. Fairbanks got a job doing bits and understudying in his touring company. He went on for the first time as "a lackey" in something called *The Duke's Jester* and Warde, in the title role, began to get nervous whenever the script called for him to ring for his servant, since Fairbanks was wont to vary his entrances—one time through a window, another time from the ceiling, only rarely from the wings as he was supposed to. His big chance came in Duluth where he went on as Laertes in *Hamlet* on short notice. "Mr. Warde's supporting company was bad, but worst of all was Douglas Fairbanks," the local critic wrote. Warde himself was to call the young actor's first season "a catch-as-catch-can encounter with the immortal bard." He discharged him at the end of the tour with the advice that he gain more experience of the world so that he could place less reliance on his undisciplined imagination when interpreting a role and more on observed reality.

Fairbanks, despite his passion for the theater, was glad to oblige, for he was always as restless as he was ambitious, and at this point he may well have wondered if the pleasures of displaying himself in public were worth the cost in self-discipline that the theater exacted. The following fall he enrolled in a "special course" at Harvard—in fact some kind of probationary status designed to see if, despite his lack of a high-school diploma, he was qualified for college. He spent most of his time in the gym, which was the best one he had ever seen.

He was, it would seem, very earnest about following Warde's advice, for Harvard, even with eccentric attendance, did not seem much like life to him. After a few months he took passage on a cattle boat to Europe—a smelly twelve-day voyage—and worked his way around the Continent. He came back and took a job in Wall Street, enjoying the opportunity it presented for sharp dressing and the exercise of his charm as a salesman, though he felt oppressed by office hours and decorum. He drifted into wholesaling hardware and then back to the stage in a touring company of *A Rose of Plymouth Town*, whose leading lady later declared that her impression was that "he had a bad case of St. Vitus's dance."

Apparently, two years of worldly experience had not notably contributed to his thespic skills, but he had established a pattern he was to repeat during his fourteen-year, on-again, off-again career on the legitimate stage. He was ever willing to take a flyer on some new occupation or simply to take off and see some new part of the world. Clearly, his dedication was not to his art, but to himself.

In theory, the theater is an ideal place for self-display. But in practice it is not always so, especially when one's roles are small and cannot be tailored, as a film star's parts can be, to the actor's special gifts and needs. Therefore, it was natural for Fairbanks to experiment with other jobs that might provide him freer rein. All his life, indeed, he demonstrated a deep need to be footloose, to get away from his routine. He was to tell later interviewers that during this time he took off for a walking tour to Cuba and a long voyage to the Orient. His son believes these were, if anything, projections of a desire for travel he was later to fulfill on a grand scale, the anecdotes with which he decorated these reminiscences drawn from later experiences. It appears that when he was "at liberty" (or working in New York) he was a fellow-traveler of New York's young socialites. Clearly, he had inherited his mother's yearnings for respectability and that must have played a part in his choice of companions. Certainly his lifelong fondness for this crowd was instrumental in his forging the first links between them and the élite of the movie world, a raffish crew who—like their predecessors in legitimate and variety theater—were not usually regarded as fit company for polite society.

Still, he was very much his own man. For as his later work would prove, he must have been keeping a close and satirical eye on his friends' manners and morals, since his first film success was in part based on his ability to make fun of their pretensions and preoccupations (nothing vicious about it, just good clean fun for the honest yeomanry who were his basic audience and whose contempt for the smart set was matched only by their envious curiosity about it).

Anyway, he drifted back and forth between the theater and his other interests, eagerly seeking something, anything, that could fully absorb his preternatural energy. The stories of his athleticism abound. On one occasion, for example, producer William Brady, who became Fairbanks' mentor, was astonished to find him filling time during a rehearsal break by walking up and down a staircase on the set on his hands.

It was Brady's wife, the actress Grace George, who apparently was the first to sense that Fairbanks (whom she had encountered working in the chorus of a Shubert musical) had, for want of a better term, star quality. "He's not good looking. But he has a world of personality—just worlds of it," she told her husband, who had already used him, without remarking his extraordinary presence, in a small part in one of his many productions. In the period 1905–1907 Fairbanks signed an exclusive contract with Brady and worked steadily for this prolific and imaginative producer, who rivaled such legendary contemporaries as Belasco, Ziegfeld, and Sam

Harris as a force on the bustling Broadway of that era. Nothing Fairbanks worked in—*A Case of Frenzied Finance, As Ye Sow, Clothes, The Man of the Hour*—was particularly memorable, though there is evidence that Brady felt he had in Fairbanks a property worth developing, for each time out his role was more important, and the last, by George Broadhurst, one of a number of playwrights attempting to bring a new realism to the American theater, was soberly received by the critics and ran for something like a year—the longest run Fairbanks had yet had in New York.

It was during his engagement in the Broadhurst play that Fairbanks met and fell in love with plump, pretty, blonde Beth Sully. There is some dispute about the immediate consequences of this match for his career. She was the daughter of Daniel J. Sully, the legendary "Cotton King," who had at one time cornered the market in that particular commodity and then, a few years before Fairbanks met his daughter, had lost a good deal of his fortune. There was still enough left to organize a huge society wedding at Kenneth Ridge, his impressive mansion at Watch Hill, R. I., and his semi-official biographer Lititia Fairbanks holds that there was still enough social pride and personal power for Sully to insist that his new son-in-law abandon his theatrical aspirations and take up honest work, setting him up as a salesman in the Buchan Soap Co., one of the many firms in which Sully held an interest. In her book *Douglas Fairbanks: The Fourth Musketeer*, she prints letters from Brady and another theatrical associate urging Fairbanks not to give up his promising career. Douglas Jr., on the other hand, insists that his father saw his season in soap as no more than a stop-gap during a short period when he simply could not find suitable roles on Broadway. He points out that his mother, Beth, had been a stage-struck girl who had abandoned most of her previous friends and interests when she fell in love with Doug and later came to pride herself on the soundness of the career advice she offered her husband. As for her family, they "rather enjoyed the new kind of . . . limelight they began to share . . . so different from that to which they had previously been accustomed." In fact, when Sully lost the remainder of his fortune a few years later, Fairbanks, his career now in the ascendancy, had to contribute to their support and some time after that, when Douglas, Jr., began his career, he also helped out.

But whether he volunteered for the soap business or was forced into it, Fairbanks attacked it with his customary high spirits, his habit being to prove the purity of the Buchan product by taking a bite out of a sample bar and cheerfully chewing on the stuff. Such heroics in the cause of wholesaling were blessedly not of long duration. The short, sharp recession of 1907–08 washed out Sully's soap business and in August, 1908, Fairbanks was back on stage. His vehicle—and his first starring role—was a short-lived Rupert Hughes concoction, *All for a Girl*. After it closed he went into what proved to be one of his longest-running successes, *A Gentleman from Mississippi*, which starred its co-author, the beloved and veteran character actor Thomas Wise, who played a shrewd old cardsharp, while Fairbanks played his equally roguish protégé and secretary. It ran for a full season, and it was during that time—on December 9, 1909—that his only child, Douglas Fairbanks, Jr., was born.

From this season until he left for Hollywood Fairbanks was almost never at liberty. *The Cub*, a revival of *Lights o' London*, *A Gentleman of Leisure*, a Chicago run in something called *Officer 666* (he switched allegiance from Brady to George M. Cohan with this production), *Hawthorne of the U.S.A.*, a revival of *The New Henrietta*—these were the forgettable works that occupied him for the next five years. Comedies and comic melodramas for the most part, they were not designed for the ages, any more than most of the movies that soon began to absorb the same audience were. They were solidly crafted light entertainments, some of which presented Fairbanks with excellent opportunities to show off his athleticism. In one, for example, he improved on a stage direction that called for him to run up a flight of stairs by vaulting, catching the overhang of a balcony and pulling himself gracefully up to the heroine's side. In another, he was required to rescue the maiden from an angry crowd, and he enthusiastically threw himself into the melee eight times a week, often emerging battered and bruised, but delighted by the improvisations forced on him by over-enthusiastic extras.

During this period Cohan wrote a vehicle for him, *Broadway Jones*, in which he promised that Doug would play a typical American youth, winning fame, fortune, and the girl against heavy odds. It was the sort of thing on which his first movie success would be built, but in the writing Cohan found the part irresistible—and cast himself in it. Fairbanks registered no complaint, apparently, and found himself in the aptly titled, *He Comes Up Smiling*. Again, it appears to have been fairly typical not only of the plays that preceded it, but also the movies that would shortly succeed it. It was about a bank clerk bored with his job who undertakes a life of adventurous vagabondage and, after many cheery thrills, finds fortune and romance. The *New York Times* called it "a gay story of a great adventure" and noted that Fairbanks' performance "justified" his star billing. Another publication said that he romped through it so gaily that "one almost overlooks the fact that he is getting to be more than a pleasant personality and is doing some real acting."

He Comes Up Smiling did not for long add to the gaiety of

nations. It ran only a couple of months, despite the reviewers' pleasure in a role that suited the young star's emerging public image better than any he had previously had on Broadway. It is said that it failed because there were simply too many competing comedies featuring too many great names on Broadway that Fall. No matter. Fairbanks was only briefly at liberty. He almost immediately went into rehearsal for what was to be his last Broadway play, James Forbes' *The Show Shop*, a comedy about the foibles of show folks and show business and, as a satire on the pretentions of the breed and the trade, it was an appropriately breezy finale to his career on Broadway.

Not that he knew it was to be so when he opened on New Year's Eve, 1914. Indeed, he did not know it was the end of this phase of his career when the play ended its run in May, 1915, though surely he understood that he was, at last, a star—and a star of a particular kind. That is to say, he was not, and probably only occasionally (and early) aspired to be, an actor in the classic mold, a player of parts, a man willing to submerge his personality under other, "literary" personalities. No, more important than his growing fame was the fact that he had firmly established a theatrical character, a public personality, a known quantity that audiences could count on, in advance, to deliver a certain kind of entertainment. It was now the middle of 1915 and it had required all the years of the young century to impose himself on the theater, to get the kind of vehicles that were exactly right for him. All unknowing, he had been preparing himself for the greater celebrity still to come.

He didn't realize it, and the industry was not fully aware of it, but he had been creating out of the raw materials of his essential self precisely the kind of image that the movies at the moment required.

III

The history of movie stardom as an institution is a familiar one: how the producers had resisted giving billing to the actors who played in their little films; how the actors themselves, regarding appearance in a medium that robbed them of what they regarded as their prime artistic resource, the voice, had been glad to hide their shame in anonymity; how the public had begun singling them out of the crowds on the screen, demanding to know more about them, and, more important, demanding to know, in advance, which pictures featured their favorites; how a few independent producers, grasping at any weapon to fight the motion picture trust (composed of the major studios), had acceded to public opinion and been rewarded by the most deliciously rising sales curves; how the demand for stars was quickly perceived as a factor that could stabilize the industry, since this demand was predictable in a way that the demand for stories or even genres was not; how, as feature-length films established their popularity and the cost of producing these longer films required bank loans, star names came to lead the list of collateral that bankers looked upon with favor when their assistance was sought; how certain actors achieved unprecedented heights of popularity and prosperity almost over-night in the period 1915–1920; and how this phenomenon, this beginning of a new celebrity system, destroyed or crippled almost everyone caught up in it—and had, as well, a deleterious effect on the movie industry.

The instrument of Fairbanks' deliverance unto a higher plane of public awareness was a now almost forgotten "pioneer of the industry," as Hollywood's ceremonial phrase goes. Harry Aitkin, with his brother Roy, had broken in as owners of middle-western theaters and film exchanges and had then, fighting the trust, shifted into production in order to supply films for these exhibiting and distributing entities. At the moment, the Aitkins had an utterly unprecedented hit on their hands. At the end of 1913 they had signed D. W. Griffith, the industry's premier director, and, as the ad announcing his departure from that studio put it, "Producer of all great Biograph successes, revolutionizing Motion Picture drama and founding the modern technique of the art." They had won him not by outbidding their competitors on the matter of salary, but by offering profit participation and, most important to the artistically ambitious Griffith, the opportunity to make independent productions, for which they agreed to raise outside capital and to make special distribution arrangements. The first of these was *The Birth of a Nation*. It was not the world's, or the nation's, first feature-length film, not even the first *successful* one. But beside it, all competition paled, for no one had previously orchestrated all the resources of the cinema as Griffith had in this film, alternating thunderous spectacle with scenes of the most delicate intimacy. Utilizing all the wondrous cinematic techniques (close-ups and long shots, fades and dissolves and iris-ins), he had developed the movies' first recognizable personal style in the Biograph years, while at the same time telling a story that was romantic and suspenseful and, because of its unconscious but palpable racism, wildly controversial. Because the movie was distributed on a states' rights basis, and because the holders of those rights were less than forthcoming when reporting their grosses to the Aitkins, no one knows just how much the picture made, though it is likely that no film until *The Godfather*, over sixty years later, ever outgrossed it. Still, even with a great deal of cheating going on, literally millions flowed back to Griffith, the Aitkins, and others who were either entitled to a percentage of the film's profits or were shareholders in Epoch, the corporation that had been set up to handle *Birth*. Though investors in Harry Aitkin's major film companies (Reliance-Majestic, which was a production outfit, and Mutual, which was a distributor) were less than happy about this, especially since the director, stars, and technicians who worked on *Birth* were mostly under contract to these corporations and the picture had mostly been shot on a lot controlled by Reliance-Majestic, the success of the film temporarily gave Harry Aitkin the one thing he had until then lacked in his movie career—money. The day of the one- and two-reel movie (except for comedies) was over, and he now wanted to accomplish two things—establish a steady flow of longer films (four to six reels) from studio to distributor to theater and produce more spectacles of *The Birth of a Nation*'s scope. Moreover, he had given up managerial control of Mutual in exchange for some of the financing of that film and was now being squeezed by his one-time Mutual friends. It was time, he thought, to create a new distribution arm that he would control—and that might be the beginning of a production-distribution-exhibition empire such as his competitor, Adolph Zukor, was also beginning to envision.

Now, in addition to his arrangement with Griffith, he had Griffith's one-time employee, Mack Sennett, who was the country's best-known comedy director, and Thomas Ince, one of the leading producers of action films, under contract with Reliance-Majestic. So his first step was simple and shrewd. He would get them to sign with a new production company, leaving Reliance-Majestic a shell and Mutual's distribution arrangements with it virtually valueless. He succeeded, and the three director-producers joined him to form Triangle, which was both a production and a distribution company. But Aitkin knew that was not enough. For what we now call the star system had begun to take shape and by this time it was clear to businessmen that "personalities" were, most of the time, more potent as a factor in luring audiences to the theater than directors ever could be.

It had all begun in the summer of 1909 when Florence Lawrence, Griffith's original "Biograph Girl," was lured away by Carl Laemmle, another one-time exchange man who had gone into production to fight the trust (emerging eventually as the dominant figure at Universal). The Biograph players, like those employed by other members of the trust, had labored in anonymity, and the opportunity of receiving billing, the chance to build their own names, had been irresistible not only to Miss Lawrence but to everyone else then employed in this infant, if lustily growing, industry. Stars quickly became one of the most potent instruments for breaking the trust's stultifying hold on it.

The managers of the trust companies had resisted the star system for one basic reason. They had been used to paying actors as little as five dollars a day, and since the typical one-reeler rarely required more than a day or two to shoot, they were getting actors to play leads for the merest pittance. They quite correctly foresaw that if they were allowed billing, the most popular of these players could literally capitalize on their names and that their demands would turn the movies into a high-risk business. Who knew where it might end? You might find yourself paying some slip of a girl $75 or $100 a week. What they did not foresee was that such figures would be quickly surpassed, and that the stars would, in most instances, be worth every penny of their astronomical salaries.

The great pioneers of this aspect of the industry were Mary Pickford, whom Fairbanks was shortly to meet, and Charles Chaplin, who was to be their friend and founding partner in United

Artists. Of the two, it was Miss Pickford who was most assiduous in her cultivation of stardom's economic potential. Like nearly every major movie actor of this first generation (Fairbanks, Chaplin, The Gish sisters, Mae Marsh, Blanche Sweet, Bobby Harron, to name but a few), she was the child of a broken home and like most of them she went into the theater as a child, not out of any great desire for self-expression, but in order to help support her family. It had not been an easy life. Even with her mother, sister and (later) brother also trouping, they had barely scraped together a living. So from the start, her drive to find financial security was powerful, more so than that of any of her contemporaries. On the very day in 1909 when she applied to Griffith at Biograph for work, she managed to talk him into doubling the going rate for day work (to $10) and within a short time she was getting a guarantee of $25 a week against three days' work, extra days to be compensated at $10 each—an unprecedented arrangement at that niggardly studio. She departed in 1911 to put in a year with another company at $175 a week, though in this one instance her move was dictated less by the desire to achieve greater economic rewards than by the chance to work with Owen Moore, one of Griffith's leading men, whom she had married against her mother's wishes—a step she lived to profoundly regret. Thereafter, she returned to Griffith for another year, left again to do a play, *A Good Little Devil*, for David Belasco and found herself under contract to that pioneer of the star system, Adolph Zukor, then organizing his Famous Players ("in Famous Plays," to complete the slogan). The film version of *Little Devil* was not especially successful, nor was Zukor's basic idea of making film versions of plays using the stars of the legitimate stage. Most of them couldn't seem to get the hang of screen acting and, anyway, the public liked the younger, fresher faces Griffith in particular had been bringing to the movies. Little Mary, however, already had a huge following among the movie audience and they welcomed her back. By 1914 Zukor was paying her $1,000 a week and staved off a competitor's offer of twice that amount by conducting a negotiating session in a tearoom on Broadway late in the afternoon. When darkness fell and the lights came on he was able to show Miss Pickford that actor's dream of glory—her name in lights on Broadway.

That didn't satisfy her for long. In a very short time her salary went to $2,000 a week, then to $4,000, finally to $10,000—all against 50 per cent of the gross. Yet she could honestly claim she was underpaid, given the contribution she made to the economic welfare of Famous Players and its successor, Famous Players-Lasky, which in turn, in time, became the nucleus of Paramount Pictures. One of the partners in the second firm, Samuel Goldwyn, might sourly note that it took longer to make one of Mary's contracts than it did to make one of her pictures, but the fact was that her value, in these first star-struck moments, was incalculable. Sure of her own worth and sure that she knew best how to maximize it, she led the movement toward independent production, in which stars would attempt to be the dominant creative force in the making of their own films—choosing stories, co-stars, directors. It was to obtain this power that she left Zukor in 1918 to head her own unit distributing through First National, a concern organized by the exhibitors, and, of course, she was a prime mover in the formation of United Artists a couple of years later, when she felt she still had not obtained full control of her destiny.

What did she represent to the mass audience? It is hard for people to understand her incredible appeal nowadays, when she lives a virtual recluse in Pickfair, her films largely unshown, even in the museums. It is hard to reconcile the hard-driving business-woman of everybody's memoirs (including her own) with the image that has come down to us, that of a cloyingly sweet optimist, playing little-girl roles until she was in her thirties. That image is, however, erroneous. Her screen persona was certainly optimistic but even in *Pollyanna*, the movie many people believe—again wrongly —was most characteristic of her work, she was not by any means a figure of mindless cheer. Indeed, she came to hate the film and at the time she was working on it did her best to give her character some other dimensions. For example, in her autobiography she tells of a fly that buzzed into camera range one day while she was working. "Little fly, do you want to go to heaven?" she sweetly inquired. With that she caught it, clapped her hands together and said, "You have." Whether there actually was a fly there is hard to determine from the film itself, but the business—and the subtitles reflecting her improvisation—are.

Indeed, she played the entire role with a delicious sense of irony and here, as elsewhere, her character proved to be spunky and inventive when danger threatened or trouble loomed. Because of her golden curls and her tiny frame, audiences tended to sentimentalize her, but she rarely sentimentalized herself. She tried hard to break out of the trap that audience expectations became (as when she played not only Little Lord Fauntleroy, but his mother as well, as early as 1921). She was, indeed, as fine an actress—delicate in her pantomime, a realistic underplayer—as the silent screen ever produced. Perhaps more to the point in considering the rage over her, she represented an interesting transitional figure. Beginning her career at the end of a long era in which the stage and literature had grossly romanticized and sentimentalized childhood, she partook of what remained of that feeling ("Did we, perhaps, interpret you to yourself, and is 'Our Mary' our creation as well as yours?" Edward Wagenknecht once shrewdly inquired in an open letter to her), yet she gently moved the crowd a step or two beyond the old pieties, easing them toward a slightly truer—if still idealized—understanding of childhood and adolescence.

One cannot claim that this was a conscious creative act on her part. Her career, like that of every great star, was in part a lucky accident. She was, among other things, simply the right person at the right time and place to encapsulate and symbolize something in the spirit of her historical moment. By 1917 she would collect over a million votes in a star popularity poll conducted by a woman's magazine, outdistancing her nearest competitor by over a half-million votes. In that same year Vachel Lindsay, the movie-mad poet, would write, "To reject this girl in haste is high treason to the national heart." She would even get the flu at the right time and when, in 1919, the great epidemic swept the world, carrying off more victims than World War One had, it was Little Mary the populace worried about, fretting about her sickness, as one newspaper put it, "as devotedly and sympathetically as if it were a personal sorrow."

It begins to seem that her romance with Douglas Fairbanks was somehow preordained, for he was, personally and professionally, cut from much the same cloth—that cheerful, stubborn, shrewd, and optimistic man, who was also a transitional figure, demonstrating how old values might be preserved in new times. That, though, is getting ahead of the story. For now, in the spring of 1915, it was sufficient for operators like Harry Aitkin to note that Miss Pickford was getting $2,000 a week, that Charles Chaplin was receiving $1,250 a week plus a $10,000 bonus for signing with Essanay (in a year he would be getting $670,000 a year—with a

$150,000 bonus on signing—from Mutual and by 1918 he would sign his famous million-dollar contract with First National). Obviously something unprecedented was in the air. The screen gave actors, in the month or two of a film's release, exposure of a kind they could not achieve in a lifetime of touring. Moreover, it was an intimate and realistic (or at least realistic-*seeming*) medium. People actually thought they knew these people, these new stars, right down to their smallest habits and mannerisms, in a way they had never known any other public figures. They identified with them in a new and more direct way than had ever been the case with other actors or other heroes—political, military, social.

Everyone was surprised, not least the recipients of this new adulation. It would take them some years to adjust to it, to make rational arrangements for living with it and preserving some sense of privacy and true identity. Not a few would perish under it, victims of drink or drugs, of a massive shift of public opinion against them, or simply from the pressure of it all, grotesquely inflating or horribly crushing egos that were less than perfectly adaptable to magnitudinous shifts in personal status. In his autobiography Charles Chaplin discusses very movingly how it came to him that he was dealing with such a quantum change. He had taken a slow train from Los Angeles to New York to sign that $670,000 contract, and as people normally did in those days, he got off at various stops to conduct business by telegraph. The word passed up the line, from one operator to another, that Chaplin was on the train and from them it trickled out to the general public. At each long stop he was besieged by larger and larger crowds, and, in Chicago, he required a police escort to move from one depot to another. In New York he debarked at 125th Street rather than face the mob at Grand Central. The contract was front-page news, and a stunned and benumbed Chaplin aimlessly wandered the streets, his mood vacillating between elation and despair. "Now I am alone," he said to himself, quoting Hamlet. His thoughts on that occasion have been echoed ever since by victor-victims of the American celebrity system: "How does one get to know people, interesting people? It seemed that everyone knew me, but I knew no one."

It is a strange and terrible thing, this alienation peculiar to the celebrity, that Chaplin was among the first to feel. Perhaps a few great literary figures of the nineteenth century, men like Lord Byron, and later, people like Dickens and Mark Twain, who had chosen to go before the public as lecturers, had known something like it, but no other artists had ever been subjected to its peculiar ironies simply because the technology of high-speed mass communication (including movies themselves) had not existed before. And this support system, to borrow another more recent phrase, is a requisite of celebrity as we now define it.

The ironies are rich, unbearably so. The basic one, of course, is that the celebrity's wealth, his continuing strength, always depends on the favor of the crowd, whose simple adulation feeds a desperate desire to share the celebrity's living presence (as if, somehow, that could solve the mystery of their attraction to him or permit them to partake magically of his imagined strength). This, in turn, must drive the celebrity to run from what is, after all, the source of his power. Worse, he must know, in some corner of his mind, that he is like them in some way, or else he would not elicit such powerful feelings. In short, he lives in a constant state of ambivalence toward his public, alternately courting it and despising it and, of course, seeking—usually fruitlessly—friends, employees, systems to stabilize his relationship with it and thus stabilize his own emotions. Indeed, in his brother Sidney, Chaplin had already found the nucleus of his entourage, and in his identification of himself, by the critics and intellectuals, as the movies' first great performing artist (Griffith, of course, had already been identified as their first great creator), he had the beginnings of a protective persona. But at this stage the celebrity system, like the star system which is such an important part of it, was still embryonic, its future dimensions unimaginable.

IV

Certainly in the spring of 1915 Douglas Fairbanks could not have known what he was getting into when Harry Aitkin offered him a contract with his new Triangle Pictures firm. Aitkin, like Zukor before him, was sweeping the New York stage for names and in this period signed some sixty well-known legitimate stars, among them Sir Herbert Beerbohm Tree, DeWolf Hopper, Billie Burke, Texas Guinan, and Weber and Fields. Fairbanks did not, of course, rank with them in national fame, but he was one of the most highly paid younger stage stars; to obtain his services Aitkin had to offer him a thousand a week. Even at that, Fairbanks hesitated, confessing to his friend Frank Case, owner of the Algonquin Hotel, where he and his family lived in New York, that he feared some loss of prestige if he joined the great trek to Hollywood. Still, summer was coming on and he had nothing better to do. Moreover, according to his son, he had never been farther west than Colorado and was curious about the Pacific slope. (His interest in Western history and art abided, and he would become an avid collector of the paintings of Remington and Russell.) And, as long as all these other legitimate actors seemed willing to try this experiment. . . .

So it was done. And the large salary did much to compensate for the fact that Griffith, in whose unit he was placed, couldn't figure out what to do with him. Fairbanks' bounding energy and breezy personal style irritated the humorless master, who was, in any case, preoccupied with the creation of his second, incredibly complex, masterpiece, *Intolerance.* Moreover, it should be noted that one of the tragedies of his career was that Griffith, though he had an uncanny eye for feminine screen talent (in addition to Pickford, the Gish sisters, Mae Marsh, and Blanche Sweet all began their careers with him), was, it would seem, quite uncomprehending about what constituted star quality in men. (He was later to have Rudolph Valentino in his employ and entirely miss his appeal, casting him as a villain.) For the most part his taste ran to collar-ad handsomeness coupled with a certain stiffness of manner. The best male actors he employed—Henry Walthall, Robert Harron, Richard Barthelmess—avoided these defects, but none of them was a powerful personality. The simplest explanation for this blind spot is that Griffith wanted no competition for dominance on his sets. But there is also the possibility that he had some deeper distrust of male sexuality; why else did he so often present men as lustful beasts bent on the rape of his golden-haired child-women?

In short, Fairbanks presented a problem to Griffith, and it was not eased by his habit of imitating the director's pompously drawling manner of speech and of addressing his often worshipful fellow players as if he were a *pater familias.* ("Come on, boys and girls—to work.") An eyewitness recalls the bored and restless Fairbanks working out in the gym he had created for himself on the lot, perhaps consoling himself with the thought that quite a few of his fellow players from New York were similarly underutilized and lacked his gift for keeping himself amused and fit. Still, they represented a huge investment to Aitkin, who was determined to realize something on it, even though he probably understood by this time what Zukor had also discovered: that stage stardom was not necessarily transferable to the screen. Youth and naturalism of style were the desiderata for actors in the new medium, and those were commodities in short supply among the Broadway strangers. In any case, the movie people, long the objects of contempt on the part of legit actors, were at some pains to turn the tables on them. They understood the new techniques and technology of film, and the haughty strangers had to apply to them for admission to this new fraternity—and be prepared for a certain amount of hazing.

After a summer of idleness Fairbanks was finally given something to do—a script (author unknown) called *The Lamb*, based on *The New Henrietta*, the Broadway comedy in which he had appeared. Christy Cabanne, a long-time Griffith assistant, directed while D. W. "supervised" from as great a distance as he could. Despite claims to the contrary put forward on behalf of Anita Loos and her director husband, John Emerson, a great deal of Fairbanks' essential screen personality was set forth in this first film. It was the tale of an effete Eastern snob invited to join a house party in the Wild West and forced, through a chain of unlikely circumstances, to rescue and defend Seena Owen, playing the girl who scorns his love, from marauding Indians. This was a transformation that fascinated Fairbanks. In one after the other of his short, early films he was a sissy or a seriously inhibited youth who found within himself the surprising resources to rise to difficult challenges. Even when he began rummaging through history for stories, the character he chose to play often used the role of the unconcerned, uninvolved playboy as a way of disguising his true, heroic nature (see *The Mark of Zorro*, for instance). Perhaps Fairbanks believed that he effected a similar transformation himself when he escaped from the respectability his mother had sought to impose upon him.

At this point, however, no one saw what he was driving at. On the set of *The Lamb* he irritated the crew with his irrepressible between-takes gymnastics, and they retaliated by giving him a make-up that made him appear to be a victim of anemia. Griffith was appalled and puzzled when he viewed a rough cut of the film. It may be that he focused on Fairbanks' great defect as a performer, described by George Pratt, the astute film historian, as the "self-consciousness that plagued him all his career." He adds, "Much as I enjoy him, I can see that—like some male dancers—he doesn't trust his face, knows his body will work better for him." It was the kind of thing that would bother Griffith, whose great gift with actors was capturing subtle shifts of emotion as they registered in their expressions. Anyway, a man who was present recalls Griffith asking rhetorically, "What the hell am I going to do with him?" This witness, a press agent, thought, probably correctly, that the difference between actor and director was more a matter of tempo than of temperament. As everyone knows, Griffith was the screen's first great master of suspense, building gripping climaxes through cross-cutting between imperiled heroes and heroines and those riding to their rescue. But he tended to build quite slowly to these sequences, pausing over details in the early sections of his films, revealing character through them. John Ford, the great director, who as an extra had ridden with the Klan in *Birth*, believed that Griffith's genius found its fullest expression in this careful detail work. That, however, was not where Fairbanks' genius lay. He liked to get on with the story and, more important, get on to the scenes where he could strut his stuff. He could sustain those scenes endlessly, but the individual elements of them passed in a twinkling. Fairbanks was hurt by Griffith's criticism and by his suggestion that the actor might find a more congenial home in Mack Sennett's unit, where they were . . . well, more physical.

The idea did not appeal. Indeed, one can't help but wonder if it was not intended as a none-too-subtle put-down. For Fairbanks was a reputable stage actor and however highly we may now value Sennett's work, the fact remains that he did not recruit from Fairbanks' echelon of the theater. Many of his people had been little more than roustabouts when they came to him, and none, certainly, had worked on any stage grander than that of a vaudeville house. For an actor as sensitive to gradations in social status as Fairbanks was, the idea must have been particularly galling. And, of course, it was ridiculous. Fairbanks was a splendid comedian, but he was never a knockabout *farceur*.

In the end, Griffith proposed that *The Lamb* be cut by a couple of reels, and he wired Aitkin in New York that it would require a fast-paced score to enliven audience interest. That done, he swept it out of mind and went back to brooding over *Intolerance*, his "Sun Play of the Ages," which had grown from a little four-reel story about social injustice (called *The Mother and the Law*) into an epic of unprecedented grandeur—and expense. *The Lamb* was shipped to New York in due course and Fairbanks followed, pretty well convinced he had no future in the movies.

Nevertheless, *The Lamb* turned out to be necessary for a consequential event in film history—the first attempt by anyone to charge admission prices comparable to those of a stage attraction for ordinary, program movies. For this experiment (the top price was three dollars) Aitkin wanted something by each of the Triangle producers, and Fairbanks' picture turned out to be the best thing available from the Griffith unit which, in its preoccupation with *Intolerance*, had fallen well behind in its production of bread-and-butter films. Sitting down with *The Lamb* on the night of September 23, 1915, were such lions from New York artistic circles as Paderewski, painter Howard Chandler Christy, writers Rupert Hughes and Irvin Cobb—and, as it happened, they were amused. So was the press, which proclaimed Fairbanks a very satisfactory hero.

He returned to Hollywood more irrepressible than ever. On the trip back he had been accompanied by Frank Case, the hotelman, and he had amused himself by dressing in full Indian regalia to waken Case from his slumbers one night. After he got over his fright, Case retaliated by telling the porter that Fairbanks was a mental case on a strict diet and that his frequent requests for fruit, candy, ice-cream, and other amenities were to be sternly ignored. Fairbanks doted on this sort of adolescent japery, and he and his companions devoted untold hours to elaborate practical jokes. Indeed, in later years, Fairbanks had a chair in his office wired so that he could administer electric shocks to unwary visitors, and much effort was devoted to maneuvering the unwary into the hot seat.

As of the fall of 1915, Griffith was not willing to concede star status to Fairbanks, however successful *The Lamb* was. He approved another Cabanne project, *Double Trouble* (with Fairbanks playing twins), and still found his sense of decorum offended by the actor. It was at that point that an even less highly regarded stage hand took a hand. His name was John Emerson, and he had been a friend of Fairbanks' in New York. On the coast he had switched from acting to directing. He asked for a chance to do something with his old pal, and although Griffith warned him off—"Don't waste your time, Emerson, because that man can't act"—he put no real obstacles in his way. After all, they might as well keep Fairbanks busy until his contract ran out. Rummaging around in the files kept by Frank (Daddy) Woods, Griffith's shrewd story editor, Emerson discovered a bundle of comedy scenarios by a very young girl named Anita Loos and returned to The Master excited by their possibilities as Fairbanks vehicles. Griffith was again unenthusiastic. "Don't let that material fool you," he said, "because the laughs are all in the lines; there's no way to get them onto the screen."

Why couldn't the gags be printed as subtitles, Emerson wondered. Because, said Griffith, people don't go to the movies to read—they go to look at pictures. Why, then Emerson inquired, had Griffith purchased these scripts? "I like to read them myself," he replied. "They make me laugh."

Perhaps Griffith perceived a certain illogic in his position as he enunciated it. He was, after all, a man who loved flowery, pseudopoetic subtitles and was often guilty himself of overloading his films with them. Or perhaps, still preoccupied with *Intolerance*, he was merely seeking another temporary solution to the nagging Fairbanks problem. Anyway, he told Emerson to meet with Miss Loos (eventually they were to extend their collaboration into marriage) and she was easily persuaded to add more gags, visual and verbal, to the scenario. Fairbanks, according to his son, "approved—enthusiastically—of the collaboration with Emerson and Miss Loos." He insists, however, that "although they worked very closely together, the final decision as to what to do always rested with him." *The Lamb*, and its immediate successor, *Double Trouble*, were, according to the younger Fairbanks, the only films his father ever made in which he was not the *de facto* "boss" of the production. He was, in short, lucky that Griffith was occupied elsewhere, for at this time Chaplin and Pickford were the only performers to have similar control over their film appearances. He was also lucky to find collaborators obliging enough to let him set the pace of these early movies, which firmly fixed his image with the public. Had Griffith, for example, taken personal control of the Fairbanks films, there would have been a fierce fight for dominance, for the director believed in the repertory concept, partly because of theatrical idealism, partly because it insured that in his films the director—himself—would remain the star. (When the players he developed were offered starring contracts elsewhere he always let them go with a regretful little speech, making no attempt to match competitors' offers.) In the short run, of course, he was wrong. Very quickly stars would dominate the public's consciousness, be the most valuable "properties" in the studios' inventories, and the absence of major names in his films would hurt him at the box office. In the long run, perhaps, he has been proved còrrect. Star salaries, especially in the last troubled quarter century of American movie history, have been a significant fact in driving production costs to uneconomic heights. And, since they bear no conceivable relationship to the actual value of an actor's services, they must be troubling psychologically to many who receive them. Who can, in reality, live up to the huge prices set upon his person? Who can be anything but anxious that a capricious fate, having dumped riches of a magnitude that no one can be said to deserve, might not just as capriciously take them away? Who can feel anything but alienation from the ordinary masses, whose adulation must be mixed with a threatening envy, and who certainly cannot be expected to understand the problems of the overrewarded?

At the time, of course, Fairbanks understood nothing of this.

One must imagine him as grateful for collaborators who understood his essence, and could help him to bring it out in dramatic form. The formula that Loos, Emerson, and Fairbanks hit upon was actually quite a simple one. She did, indeed, get more wit into the subtitles than had been present in his previous film, and Emerson had the good sense, as Alistair Cooke was to put it, "to let Fairbanks' own restlessness set the pace of the shooting and his gymnastics to be the true improvisations on a simple scenario." Not, of course, that the stunts were as easy as Fairbanks made them look. "They were, in fact, all carefully planned and rehearsed over a considerable period beforehand," his son says. "He would design and work on them, extending their scope, for days and weeks ahead, until he was capable of doing them on a much bigger scale than was actually to be photographed later on."

At all events, the new team had a high old time shooting their first film together. Titled *His Picture in the Papers*, it was quickly finished and even more quickly disapproved by Griffith, who again thought it had no future as a feature. Perhaps, he suggested again, it could be cut to a two-reel comedy—a strategy, which would also again have resulted in considerable loss of status for Fairbanks. And so an impasse was reached and the film was shelved. Or so everyone thought. But as with *The Lamb*, a print was somehow shipped to New York anyway and, in turn, it was sent over to Roxy Rothafel at the Strand theater as a substitute for a picture he had booked but which had got lost in transit. By the end of the first reel of *His Picture* the theater, according to Miss Loos, "was fairly rocking with laughter." By the next day *The New York Times* had proclaimed it a hit, and Roxy, of course, kept it on.

In the Loos-Emerson plot formula, all the "acting" took place in the early going when Fairbanks might be discovered, in monocle and spats, idling about some mansion or watering place, good-natured but a figure of fun to everyone but himself. As a variation, he might be seen as a repressed or inhibited dreamer, trapped in some routine job and longing for adventure. The point was simply to set up a situation where the true Fairbanks—resourceful, daring, gallant—could emerge from an improbable cocoon and demonstrate his remarkable heroic gifts. In that very first Loos-Emerson film, for example, he was seen in a long match with a professional boxer, dove from the deck of an ocean liner into the sea, and took a mighty leap from a speeding train. In subsequent films he was to be observed fighting forest fires, climbing the sheer walls of canyons, and being a "human submarine." In many of these five-reel films the American West, the West of Fairbanks' boyhood, served, as Alistair Cooke said, as "an antidote, a goal for the fretting city worker to aim at . . . as a source of natural virtue."

The first half of the typical Fairbanks film, then, established audience identification with him. Occasionally, as a subtitle in *The Americano* put it, he was "an all-around chap, just a regular American." But more often he was something less than that; one actually felt sorry for him, cut off, a poor little rich boy to whom the simple, hearty joys of ordinary life, not to mention the richer pleasures of plain-spoken masculinity, were denied. Which, of course, made his eventual breakthrough to normalcy all the more satisfying. Man is great, wrote Emerson, "not in his goals, but in his transitions"—a very American thought and one which, it is fair to speculate, was much on the nation's mind (if mostly subconsciously so) at the time. Before the nation was the example of a Europe in what appeared to be its death throes, and it was understood that there was something singular in the American experience, the

American character, that permitted us to escape the Continental fate. We had, a nation of transplanted Europeans, made a great transition and were entitled to be proud of it. On the other hand, the world was perceptibly entering upon a period of enormous change, mostly technological in its basis (with the movies an excellent example of this new technology), and it needed to be shown that these new transitions could be managed gracefully. Rich or poor, the Fairbanks character was, in these early films, essentially an urban type, and it was important to show not only that he could handle the problems presented by modern cities and the inventions that made them functional, but that he could, with a little effort, master the traditional skills of the frontiersman, now rapidly receding to mythical status. And overriding all of this was yet another correlation with one of the basic sets of the American mind. Some years ago, commenting briefly on Fairbanks, I wrote: "If . . . the basic concern of Americans is not with end product, but with process, then it was at the moment of [his athletic] improvisations that Fairbanks achieved greatness in our eyes." A room, as Alistair Cooke so nicely put it, was "a machine for escape" and to see Doug at bay and fighting off his enemies the while casing the joint for possibilities—that staircase, there, that balcony yonder, that chandelier above, how can I put them together to befuddle these fools?—this was the moment of high deliciousness in all his work. The possibilities were always obvious to his audience, but not the sequence of their employment, nor the variations he could ring on a simple action (who else, for example, would have thought of, let alone dared, a handspring powered and supported by only one arm?). Lightning pragmatism, that was the heart of his style, and the combination of the national obsession with quickness and the nation's only major contribution to philosophy was no trivial invention. Its appeal abides—perhaps better than the relentless optimism of his nature.

V

God knows, he naturally looked on the bright side of things, and in the first flush of his fame it was the role of the optimist that came naturally to him and, indeed, had its uses. "At a difficult time in American history," Cooke wrote, "Douglas Fairbanks appeared to know all the answers"—and gave them with a great absence of pretentiousness. And not just to interviewers. For here, as elsewhere, he pioneered new territory for the celebrity system, permitting his name to be affixed to a monthly column in *Photoplay*, one of the many new magazines that had sprung up to answer the public's need for information about this new breed, the movie stars—a need that was distinctly not being fully answered by the more traditional journalism. In time, there were peppy books— *Laugh and Live, Make Life Worth-while, Whistle and Hoe—Sing as We Go*—to name just some of his titles. Aimed at what we would now call "the Youth Market," they were produced by his secretary and confidant, Kenneth Davenport, an early member of the star's obligatory entourage, whose inclusion therein was the result of a typically expansive gesture on the star's part. Davenport had acted in one of Fairbanks' Broadway shows, the star had borrowed an overcoat from him one night, and Davenport had taken a chill going without it. He was diagnosed, shortly thereafter, as tubercular, though it is doubtful, of course, that there was a cause-effect relationship between the borrowed overcoat and the contracting of so major an illness. Fairbanks chose to think otherwise, however, and when the opportunity arose, put Davenport on the payroll. His style cannot be accounted distinguished. "I am not much given to preaching," he had Fairbanks say in one typical column, "but if I ever took it up as a vocation, I would preach cleanliness first and most." And, repetitively: "The boy who wishes to get to the front in athletics must adopt a program of mental and bodily cleanliness." And, as a sort of peroration: "Perhaps the greatest foe to athletic success among young college men is strong drink. Personally I have never tasted liquor of any sort." Modestly he disclaimed great virtue for this negative achievement, calling attention to the pledge his mother had made him take and handsomely giving more credit to "the person who has fallen under its influence and fought his way out. . . ."

Banal stuff. But the quality of Fairbanks' thoughts on the alcohol problem is not at issue here. The point is that booze represented a major social problem in the United States at the time, similar in its emotional potency to marijuana in our own time. We are, by this time, used to movie stars and persons engaged in similarly light-minded occupations pontificating on serious matters, but in the teens of this century it was unprecedented, a beginning of a kind of intellectual desegregation of the actor—the humble, strolling player, of perhaps dubious value in his own falsely modest view—and of those who make their living as political and social commentators. Anyway, there is a clear line from Fairbanks' innocent pronouncement on clean living to such politicized actors as John Wayne on the right and Marlon Brando on the left. And, of course, it raises some interesting questions. Does their glamour lend their views an enchantment for the public in excess of the quality of those views? Or does the public, or at least the most significant segments of it, discredit them unfairly because they are, after all, merely actors, ever suspect of role-playing? And what about those actors like Ronald Reagan and George Murphy, their minor movie careers washed up, who use what's left of their appeal to vault into public offices for which, by any reasonable standard, they are unqualified? Or is it possible their careers may be exemplary? Does not their success make a mockery of the pretense that we actually apply reasonable standards to the process of choosing our political leaders? Finally, what about politicians like John Lindsay, self-confessedly a frustrated actor, who surround themselves with show-biz figures and who, indeed, comport themselves more like movie stars, flashing their mod clothes, their dentistry adazzle, on the talk shows in an effort to build national constituencies to which, on the basis of their performance in office, they are not strictly entitled?

Amusing speculations. Especially in light of the fact that slightly before Fairbanks launched himself in this new direction, Mary Pickford was offered a contract equal in value to her movie contract by an advertising agency which wanted to use her for endorsements of harmless commercial products. In her autobiography she quotes her attorney, Dennis F. ("Cap") O'Brien, later to be a key figure in United Artists and perhaps the first great Hollywood legal power, as saying it was an undignified and risky offer. "In time you may find your name being bandied about in all sorts of good, bad, and indifferent commercial projects . . . Your name should stand for motion pictures and not as an advertisement for evening gowns, cosmetics, and perhaps less alluring products of business."

She came to agree with him, adding: "That day I set a pattern in my life and my career which I have followed all my life."

Nor was it an unusual one. For among this first generation of stars, the basic defense improvised against the assaults of the celebrity system was an insistence on their identity as artists. Traditionally, of course, artists had never had any truck with commerce other than that directly connected with their art and, aside from literary men, had ventured few if any political or social opinions in public. As early as 1840 Thomas Carlyle had specifically included both the poet and the man of letters among the divinities, prophets, priests, and kings that were the subjects of his famous lectures *On Heroes, Hero Worship and the Heroic in History* because there was "a sacredness" about their calling. The man of letters was, he thought, "The world's priest . . . guiding it like a Sacred Pillar of Fire in its dark pilgrimage through the waste of Time." No other artists were included in his pantheon (certainly not actors) but most writers, whether they have read Carlyle or not, have followed his line, though there is opposition to it, especially among modernists. The point here is that the commercialized or politicized star-celebrity was breaking with precedent and, in the latter instance, of course, elevating himself to precisely the kind of heroic status as moral guide that Carlyle accorded his own profession—and would have been appalled to see mere actors claiming for themselves. And many, like Miss Pickford, Lillian Gish, and William S. Hart continued that sensible policy. Even Chaplin, severely and unfairly punished by public opinion when he later lent his name and presence to the idealogues, always attempted to maintain a distinction between himself as artist and political man. Unfortunately, it was impossible to foresee, as the celebrity system came into being, how powerful would be the pressures of the age toward politicization, how irresistibly tempting they would be for the celebrated, how blurry the line between heroic screen images and general cultural heroism would become.

VI

A major movie star is, of course, as much art object as artist. His films are the products of many fussing hands and so is the image of the private man, created out of interviews, gossip, and public appearances. The roles he plays in his movies naturally have their significance within the frame of the film for which his performance is created. But they also have another kind of significance—as incidents in the larger drama of the star's life and career. Fairbanks, despite his natural ebullience, was, according to his son, "In so many odd ways . . . a conventional neo-Victorian, particularly in his attitudes toward manners and mores. If facets of his personal 'life style' disclosed a touch of hypocrisy, I think one might call it '*sincere* hypocrisy' . . . He felt very strongly (until his domestic troubles contradicted him) that 'respectability' was a cloak to be worn by anyone in serious public life." There were, of course, factors other than domestic trouble complicating this matter for Fairbanks—these factors, indeed, are the main subject of this book—but it is doubtless true that it was with the beginning of marital difficulties, difficulties that threatened not only the public's rather limited and complacent understanding of who he was and what he represented, that Fairbanks began to see that his new and wondrously prosperous career was going to entail more than just making good, amusing films.

Outwardly, in the years between 1915 and 1918, when Fairbanks and his first wife were divorced, everything went swimmingly for Doug. In 1917 a peak in one of the national parks had been unprecedentedly named for him and by the time he had finished his contract with Triangle (and thirteen pictures all told) he was making something like $10,000 a week, though he was acutely conscious that the studio was making millions. He therefore acquired his own lot and made a distribution deal with Artcraft (a subsidiary of Famous Players-Lasky, set up to give leading talent—Griffith also briefly distributed through it—independence and a degree of autonomy). At the same time the entourage expanded with enormous rapidity. The Emerson-Loos team came with him to Douglas Fairbanks Productions and were doubtless next to the star in importance to its success. Nor could the crusty, independent, and talented Allan Dwan, who came over a little later to direct several of his films, be considered a hanger-on. But then there were the others—his brother, Robert, functioning as general manager; a man named Bennie Zeidman, personal publicist and agreeable pal; Tom Geraghty, a writer and jokester; Bull Montana, the wrestler who did comic roles for Fairbanks and even had a comedy career of sorts on his own a little later; sundry other small-parts players and general factotums. No doubt many of them were competent in their work, but it is also true that their larger function was certainly to condition the air around the master so that it was ever just the right temperature and humidity. It is one of the permanent answers to the problem of loneliness that Chaplin alluded to, and one which occurs to each new-minted celebrity with the force of an original discovery. Especially when the source of one's power is that distant abstraction, the mass audience, it is essential to have real people near at hand, ready to do your bidding without question, yet supporting the illusion that they are freely giving friends, not mere courtiers. It is a form of reassurance that power must have, will have, no matter what.

And Fairbanks and his team were incredibly successful. In 1917 they made five films—and, it is said, a million dollars for his new corporation. There were seven more pictures the next year and one more in 1919, when United Artists was formed and he took his company into that group as well as into new creative directions. In this period he took to writing many of his scenarios and even directed one (*Arizona*, judged to be the poorest of the lot). So far as one can tell, there wasn't a financial flop among them. Toward the end of his Artcraft contract he occasionally abandoned the convention of the major transformation (from fop or idler or dreamer) and appeared from the beginning in more or less his essential character, so winningly described by Alistair Cooke: "a young, vigorous man as uncompromising as his splendid physique, unfazed by tricky problems of taste and class behavior, gallant to women, with an affection for the American scene tempered by a wink." Or as Booth Tarkington put it, "a faun who had been to Sunday school."

He seemed to be handling success with the same grace he applied to his on-screen athletics. And, indeed, if there is anything left out of Cooke's description it is due recognition of this gift for grace. His traits of character—that is to say, the traits of his screen character—were so agreeable, so easy to identify with. But it was his athleticism that made him something special and unique, a truly heroic figure. For as Parker Tyler has written, "The essence of the hero may be defined as a super sort of professionalism. All men desiring greatness in the public eye . . . undergo a difficult discipline and the acquisition of an elaborate system of knowledge." Thus, however easy Fairbanks made his work appear, the audience understood implicitly that it was the product of careful planning and arduous training—a fact which was stressed in the publicity about him.

Not that he didn't get a little help from his friends. Allan Dwan, the director who worked on a number of Fairbanks' Artcraft films, has said: "He worked with speed and, basically, with grace. Stunts *per se* were of no interest to him or to me. The only thing that could possibly interest either one of us was a swift, graceful move—the thing a kid visualized in his hero." But, he added, "everything was gauged for him—we never made him strain. If he had to leap on a table to fight a duel, we'd cut the legs of that table so it would be just the leap he ought to make. He never had to reach an extra inch for anything. Otherwise, it wouldn't be graceful—it wouldn't be him and it wouldn't be right . . . Stunt men have tried to imitate him and it always looks like a stunt when they do it. With him, it always looked very natural . . ."

Off-stage, however, strains were becoming manifest. They had begun almost at the instant of his first success, when he was in New York for the opening of *The Lamb*. For it was then that he met Mary Pickford. There is both a prosaic and a romantic version of their first encounter. In the former, they were simply introduced at a party given by Frank Case. In the latter, the setting was the historic Philipse Manor in Tarrytown, New York, now carefully restored by the Rockefeller family to its appearance in colonial times, complete with functioning grist mill, but in 1915 the weekend estate of Elsie Janis, the musical comedy star whom Mary had known since she was a child when they worked together on a vaudeville bill. In this version (which has a romantic rightness about it) Fairbanks and his wife were first glimpsed by Miss Pickford as they sailed past her on the road in an open car, a leopard-skin lap robe covering them. She thought it rather ostentatious.

And certainly it was clear that she far outranked him, the moderately popular stage star, just beginning his assault on the movies, when they all settled in for the house party. Still, he was highly complimentary and she was very disappointed in her marriage to hard-drinking, ugly-spirited Owen Moore. Now, she says in her autobiography, "I was resolved to take my marital punishment with a grin. I had carved out my future in my career. It was my solace, my high fortress, where no one and nothing could molest or harm me." So she paid little heed to Fairbanks until, later in the day, she attempted to cross an icy stream on a narrow and slippery log. Halfway across, she found herself trapped, immobilized by fear. Others in the party shouted advice and comfort, but it was Douglas Fairbanks who resolved her contretemps in typical fashion—leaping on to the log, sweeping her up in his arms and nimbly depositing her on dry ground in a single graceful action.

It was, in short, a meeting that might have been invented for a scenario—both behaving in perfect public character and, indeed, they continued in character throughout the five years of courtship that followed, he avidly pursuing, she nobly resisting his advances. Or so the official historical line would have it. Actually, Fairbanks, once he had set his heart on something, was as persistent, and often as comically clever, in his pursuit of it, as any of the characters he played. And it would seem that almost from the start he had determined to contract what amounted to the movie industry's first royal marriage. For, after all, he was an actor, which is to say he was a man of immense and constantly aching ego, which the former Beth Sully could no longer assuage.

People who knew Fairbanks at this time remember the amazing lengths he went to to deceive his wife and meet Little Mary. Bennie Zeidman, for example, recalled a carefully announced fishing expedition which he and the star were supposed to be taking. It was a cover for a meeting with Miss Pickford—but on the way home they stopped at a market and bought some fresh fish to bring to Mrs. Fairbanks as proof that they had actually been innocently engaged. Anita Loos writes that Fairbanks, in order to meet Pickford, took to sleeping on a porch, well away from his wife's bedroom in their Hollywood mansion, so that after she was asleep he could slide down an ionic pillar, roll his car silently down hill before starting the motor and then speed over to Mary's house. The difficulty was getting home—pushing the car back up the hill and shinnying back up the pillar—and it is probable that no other screen actor, before or since, was fit enough to carry on such a strenuous courtship.

But what of the former Beth Sully? What had happened to render her suddenly inadequate? Everyone who knew her seems to have liked and respected her—including Miss Pickford. She was clearly a woman of strength and character. Perhaps too much so. In later years she was to say to Brian Connell, her son's biographer, "Senior always used to say I should have been his sister and not his wife, and I think it's true." He was not then—or ever—the sort of man who could be a good husband in the conventional sense of the term. He was too self-absorbed. And as a father he was a disaster. Indeed, one can't help but speculate that one source of their growing estrangement was the fact that they had a child, a child who bore his father's name. Douglas, Jr.'s memories of his father during the years he was growing up are fragmentary. There was the visit to the studio where he met his first real cowboys and Indians (and was permitted to don a war bonnet; when his mother found out, she cut his hair short against the possibility of lice); there was the time when the father loudly praised the son's bravery for stoically allowing a whole bottle of iodine to be poured into a deep cut on his knee; there was the gift of a pony the boy came to love at least as much as a demonstration that his father cared for him as for the pony itself. Mostly, however, there was only silence between them.

Beth Sully Fairbanks' recollection: "Senior was perfectly tender and nice, he just did not have the instinct of being a father. . . . He used to come into the house, day-in, day-out, and he wouldn't know the child was there. Unless I asked if he was going up to say goodnight to Douglas or unless somebody wanted to see the child, Senior displayed no interest in him—he didn't care; he was just bored."

Douglas, Jr.'s remembrance: "Up until the time my mother and father separated, I always associated him with a pleasant, energetic, and agreeable 'atmosphere' about the house, to which I was somehow attached but which was not attached to me. He also seemed to be someone I did not know very well."

So Mary Pickford cannot be regarded as a wrecker of the happy home. Once Fairbanks achieved film stardom—and perhaps before that—his home was not much more than a shell, a shelter he shared with agreeable strangers between his more important comings and goings. It was only as an advisor on his burgeoning career that his first wife retained her influence—for a while. Allan Dwan, for example, was to tell an interviewer that the first Mrs. Fairbanks had a great deal to do with her husband's choices of screen material and, in particular, Dwan remembered an incident in which she tried to talk him out of playing the title character in *The Half-Breed*, which was based on a Bret Harte story. "A dirty, filthy character and so greasy—I just don't see Doug running around that way," she said. The objection was overcome by having Fairbanks, early in the film, dive into a river, swim across, and then dry himself with leaves, taking obvious pleasure in the act—thus establishing that he took baths.

It is, of course, possible that Fairbanks resented her busying herself in his business. It is certain that he resented the tensions between his wife and his very possessive mother. Though he had sided with Beth when the latter had forced him to choose between them, it is also true that when his mother died suddenly in 1916, it was to Little Mary that he turned for comfort. She had written him a note of sympathy, he asked if he could see her, they went for a drive in Central Park, and there Fairbanks broke down and wept for the first time in his bereavement. She consoled him as best she could and when the storm passed they looked up to discover that the clock on their car's dashboard was stopped at the exact moment he began to cry. Therefore, in moments of stress they swore love or fealty to one another by invoking the phrase, "by the clock." Or so the story goes.

In any case, their affair grew in intensity from that point onward. One understands how perfect, how almost foreordained, their love must have seemed to this "very actorish, petulant, shrewd, creative man," as Dwan described him. One also understands that the marriage between Beth Sully and Douglas Fairbanks is one of many that have fallen victim to success in America and especially in American show business. She was, as Joseph L. Mankiewicz had one of his characters describe a woman of her type in *All About Eve*, "of the theater by marriage" and he has since spoken of such women very movingly. Their moment of danger, he observes, is *his* moment of triumph, the moment the husband achieves that success they have together struggled toward, sacrificed toward. For in the theater—no matter what they may feel—that moment is *his* and his alone. And, suddenly she finds most of her old functions usurped. Her one-time role as a sort of mother to his gift is filled by the audience. As Mankiewicz put it, "they'll give suck to him, spoil, scold, cuddle, and reject him in a variety of ways beyond her power even to imagine. Cooks and house-cleaners will be hired now, of course, and come and go as they do. . . ." The children will become her sole responsibility and one perhaps less valued in show business even than it is elsewhere, actors being themselves so childlike and thus both uncomprehending of the difficulties of being mothers and competitive with their own offspring.

"What else?" Mankiewicz inquires. "Partner—wailing wall—even whipping post? Forget it. What with producers, packagers, lawyers, agents, business managers, publicity men, secretaries—his professional life and income will become so compartmentalized that he, himself, will rarely know what they are. . . ."

Which leaves—sex. She learns to accept infidelity. After all, he constantly works around women whose business it is to be beautiful and desirable. So long as he comes home occasionally, the wife can teach herself to be content. But, as Mankiewicz says, "What she does dread, lives in terror of, is—serious emotional involvement on his part. It could happen any day. Her man doesn't leave of a morning, after all, for a corporate structure in which he merely fills a niche. No, this husband goes off to a fun fair where he's the brass ring on the merry-go-round. . . . He's fair game every minute he's away from home. At the studio, audition, the rehearsal—it can happen while waiting for a traffic light to change. That involvement . . . Meanwhile, back at home, the 'wife to _____' can do nothing but wait . . . for as many years as she lasts."

She is, he says, "completely helpless. Without weapons. Her physical attractions are faded; at their best they were no match for those, the best in the world, that now beguile her husband relentlessly. His former dependence upon her has been fragmented and distributed among those whose profession it is to keep him dependent. He no longer needs her. Not at all. Nor has she allies; after all, she can do nothing for anyone. Not even herself . . . She is a civilian casualty, unwept and unsung, among the theater folk."

So it was, one has to imagine, with Beth Fairbanks, the first—but not the last—victim of his celebrity, this force he had called into being, but which he, no more than anyone else who has undergone this most major of American transitions, could entirely control or predictably direct.

VII

There were, of course, obstacles to Fairbanks' performing this major act in the celebrity's rite of passage. In subsequent discussions of his momentous decision to divest himself of Beth, her wishes are not much mentioned; apparently she understood her helplessness and lack of weapons. She faded away with a nice, not exorbitant, settlement (something like $500,000), never to reappear in his life.

She remarried, hastily (and unhappily), a Pittsburgh stock-broker named James Evans. The marriage lasted a year. She tried to increase her capital by playing the market, but decreased it instead, while her father's further business reverses and the ensuing need to help him and other members of her family strained her fast-dwindling resources even more. Douglas, Jr., found himself in a bewildering variety of private schools until, finally, he and his mother decamped for Paris where, like so many expatriates of the time, they hoped the favorable exchange rate might help to slow their impoverishment. Although he there discovered that he had a gift for music, drawing, and writing, by and large it was an unhappy time for Douglas, Jr., and for his mother. It would, indeed, be something like a decade before things began to right themselves for the Fairbanks' dependents, when his own career as an actor stabilized, and Beth Sully made a happy marriage (to Jack Whiting, the musical-comedy star).

Fairbanks, meantime, was far more preoccupied by religious questions than he was by the fate of his first wife and his only child. Both he and Pickford were Catholics and thus would have to choose between religion and marriage. That was perhaps a more sobering choice for her than for him, but both feared public response not just to a divorce, which would run counter to the highly moral images they had projected, but one which would, even worse, require a public renunciation of their faiths. It was not an unreasonable fear, especially in the early years of their affair. Few, if any, had attained the heights of popular acclaim that she, in particular, had achieved. And when he joined her (and Chaplin) on that peculiar pinnacle a couple of years later, no one could sensibly judge what effect their actions might have on the crowd beneath. It was possible, if the business were mishandled, that they could lose everything. "What will my people say?" she inquired grandly of a confidant.

It irritated him. He did not like to be thwarted. The overindulged child lived on in the man. Once, asked to list his hobbies on some form or other, he had simply and cheerfully written, "Doug." Now, feeling his power and accumulating wealth, he could not understand why he might not be able to do what an anonymous citizen could easily do, and under the impress of that irony cried, "Why shouldn't I get a divorce? Caesar did it. Napoleon did it."

It was, very probably, America's entrance into World War One that both impelled them to take their chances with public opinion and gave them an edge in that gamble. They toured the country, making personal appearances in aid of a Liberty Loan drive and their love ripened with this first opportunity for prolonged and more or less open intimacy. And, together with Chaplin and others, they sold over three million dollars in bonds. This and similar uses of stars—and the movie medium itself—for patriotic, propagandistic, and morale-building purposes marked the first linkage of the new, still-undefined celebrity system with political power. In a sense, government validated the legitimacy of the movies as an important medium; celebrities as forces to be reckoned with socially. Much credit redounded to Fairbanks, Pickford, and others (especially Chaplin, whose refusal to go home to Britain and fight had caused considerable adverse comment). That alone, however, would not have enabled them to obtain their divorces so easily. Rather, as we know, there was, in the war's aftermath, a general loosening of the moral climate. There would be complaints, of course, about their match. And, within a few years, there would be a considerable backlash against what the still-influential small-town and rural American citizenry regarded as a weakening of the nation's moral fibre—much of it directed against movies and movie stars (such convenient, highly visible targets). Some of them now paid a very real price for their celebrity as the public eagerly took away what it had given, almost it seemed, as a reminder of its ultimate power.

But Doug and Mary were lucky in their timing. He quietly obtained his divorce in 1918; she got hers in March 1920 in Reno, having bought Owen Moore's silent complicity with a fat sheaf of bonds. It looked as if there was no collusion between Doug and Mary in the matter, and Mary, in fact, announced when she obtained her decree that she had no plans to marry again—although by this time the public had been allowed in on the secret of their mutual admiration. She reckoned, however, without Doug. Or perhaps she didn't. Perhaps what happened next was part of a carefully planned strategy. For Fairbanks laid mighty—and quite public—siege to her affections and word of his passion got about. It seemed terribly romantic and they married on March 28, even though her period of residence in Nevada was far short of the year then required for the granting of a divorce. The wedding ceremony was conducted at the Los Angeles home of the officiating minister; only a friend or two, Pickford's mother, Fairbank's elder brother, Jack, and his wife were in attendance. The wedding dinner was held at the house that came to be known as Pickfair—where Douglas had been living alone for a year.

If the wedding was quiet, the wedding trip was perhaps the most public the world had yet witnessed. Doug swept Mary off on a grand tour of Europe, where the crowds that greeted them were simply unprecedented in size. They were, of course, true international stars—as the stars of silent films, with no language barrier to overcome, uniquely were. Moreover, they were Americans and Americans, thanks to their timely intervention in World War One, were well liked in Europe just then. Indeed, the honeymoon turned into a triumphal procession. The lack of privacy was annoying, the size of the mobs that gathered to see them make their way through the streets staggering—and sometimes threatening.

Once, for example, while the couple was moving slowly in an open car through a great crush, on their way to a charity garden party in London, those nearest Mary laid hands on her and if her husband had not grabbed her by the ankles, she would have been pulled from the vehicle and into the crowd. Very Un-British.

Still, they *were* actors. And so chose to see all this as a comforting outpouring of love. (In Paris, Doug joyfully vaulted a barricade in a train station to greet the crowds.) They did briefly tire of mass adulation and went to Germany where, because of the war, their pictures had not been shown and they were thus unknown. After several days of anonymity they confessed their hatred of it and headed for the American occupation zone—and blessed recognition.

Their tour may well have given them some idea that the celebrity system itself, or at least the Hollywood branch, might be organized on a monarchical principle, with themselves reigning, for surely no real royalty had been granted more adulation than they were. Be that as it may, the reports of their reception abroad did them no harm at home and, indeed, people began to see in their match what Fairbanks had seen—that it was, as Alistair Cooke would later put it, "the logical finale to the Fairbanks role as popular philosopher . . . [They] came to mean more than a couple of married movie stars. They were living proof of America's chronic belief in happy endings."

VIII

Actually, the end was not yet in sight for Fairbanks and Pickford and, in the event, it would prove to be not so happy. Meantime, though, there was work to be done on all fronts. To begin with, United Artists, that good idea, was turning out to be a troubled entity in reality. It had come into being immediately before the marriage—apparently, the product of a chance remark by Oscar Price, a publicity man who had worked for William Gibbs McAdoo, Secretary of the Treasury and son-in-law of Woodrow Wilson. Price had worked on the Liberty Loan drive with the Hollywood contingent and, at some point, hearing them complain about the disparity between their salaries and the profits distributors made on their films, casually suggested they go into distribution themselves. It was, of course, an idea whose time was bound to come. But Fairbanks, ever eager to extend his contacts among those who were prominent in fields other than show business, must have been particularly intrigued by the source of the suggestion, for Price clearly had the ear of McAdoo—and McAdoo was the kind of man who had not previously been associated with the movies.

It is possible, however, that nothing would have come of the suggestion had the major producers not threatened, immediately after the end of World War One, to form some sort of combination that would sign a long-term exhibition agreement with all the major theater chains of the nation, effectively squeezing out independent production and taking away from stars and leading directors a major weapon in their salary negotiations—the threat to go independent.

Whether, in fact, the producers could have done so without

running afoul of the antitrust laws is a nice question, but Fairbanks, Pickford, and Chaplin—with William S. Hart and D. W. Griffith soon joining their discussions—decided to fight. They were the industry's major creative figures, and if they stood outside the new combine it would be denied its most powerful box-office forces. The group held an ostentatiously public organization meeting in the dining room of the Alexandria Hotel in Los Angeles, at that time the center of the movie colony's social life. They covered the tablecloth with phoney economic calculations and filled the air with big talk. Chaplin recalls producers appearing at the doorway, studying the scene, and hurrying away to discuss this new and dangerous development.

That meeting was mostly a pantomime, but there were more meetings, with lawyers and managers present, at Fairbanks' pre-Pickfair home, Greyhall.* There the outlines of United Artists began to take firmer shape. Chaplin claims his talent for business was small and his participation in this meeting nil. His brother spoke for him while he reflected, "saddened," on Little Mary's legal and business acumen. "Douglas, who assumed a debonair nonchalance, was more astute than any of us. While our lawyers haggled out legal technicalities, he would cut capers like a schoolboy—but when reading the articles of incorporation he never missed a comma."

Nor did he miss the opportunity to enlist the late Secretary of the Treasury in their plans. When the war ended McAdoo resigned

---

* The house has an interesting history. Edwardian in style, it had been built by the family that was to be Carole Lombard's godparents and patrons. During his occupancy Fairbanks added a ballroom that was used as a basketball court by subsequent occupants. Pickfair was built in Greyhall's stable area and it was often alleged, though never proved, that the two were connected by secret passages. In recent times Greyhall became actor George Hamilton's seat in Beverly Hills, connecting him with a great tradition his skills as an actor never confirmed.

from government and rented a vacation home in Santa Barbara. Passing through Los Angeles on his way there, he was greeted by a band serenading him at the station. It had been hired by Fairbanks and soon they were conferring about the new distribution company, with McAdoo agreeing to sign on as general counsel if Price could be recruited to act as president. Chaplin and Griffith agreed to join the new firm, William S. Hart declined, and early in 1919 its formation was announced.

Almost immediately it was beset by problems. For one thing, neither McAdoo nor Price had any experience in the movie business, and they were soon in conflict with their general manager, Hiram Abrams, who had come over from Famous Players. The former had attempted to enlist the backing of well-to-do friends in the building and purchasing of a chain of theaters, assuring markets for their principals' pictures. It was an expensive and time-consuming strategy and one which, in the end, proved feckless. Meantime, Pickford, Griffith, and Chaplin were still obligated, under pre-existing contracts, to provide films for other distributors and could not immediately begin producing for UA. Griffith did buy back a couple of films from First National in order to ease the company's early shortage of product and Fairbanks was able to begin work on his films at once, with Pickford following in fairly short order. Still, throughout the decade United Artists was chronically short of material to keep its exchanges busy. Moreover, Chaplin—a slow and careful worker—was never able to contribute as much to the company as the founders envisaged, while Griffith, out of tune with the times and increasingly pressed by creditors, was forced, in 1925, to take a contract with Paramount as a staff director—his UA pictures as a group having done no more than break even. Even the enormously successful films of Pickford and Fairbanks could not assure profitability for the company, especially since their greater length and more expensive production values necessarily slowed the pace at which they could be turned out. Late in the decade, the company was forced to turn to outside producers like Samuel Goldwyn (whom Little Mary never liked) and Joseph Schenck—who assumed the presidency of the company in 1924—to round out its schedules. By that time, Price and McAdoo were long gone and Abrams was pretty firmly in charge of operations. The founders became increasingly silent partners in the day-to-day operation of the concern, useful on ceremonial occasions, but essentially preoccupied with their own productions. As major stockholders in the corporation releasing their films, they were more fortunate than many latter-day stars who functioned as their own producers—they received an honest accounting from their distributor. Still, it must be said that though their UA stock did not harm Fairbanks, Pickford, and Chaplin in creating three of the first great movie fortunes, it was not for a long time a major contributor to them, either. It was only after their interests were sold in the 1950s and the corporation was completely reorganized that it finally became a truly major factor in the economic life of Hollywood.

So whatever aspirations toward tycoonship Fairbanks may have harbored were thwarted—at least in part because United Artists was a relatively small-scale operation launched at precisely the moment when the industry was going through a phase of consolidation—smaller corporations being swallowed up by the firms that would, in the classic American industrial pattern, rule the industry oligopolistically by the end of the 1920s. Still, he had his influence.

It was not accidental. And in many important respects it exceeded that of any mogul, for his power was more than economic;

it had esthetic, social, and moral dimensions as well. More important, such was the shared hold of Doug and Mary on the general public that it went unquestioned for most of the decade. The scandals that tarnished Hollywood's reputation during this period never touched them and, indeed, they were the best answer to the small-town suspicion that the movie community was, as a whole, ridden with immorality. Their marriage had an aura of serenity and stability about it that was envied without the undercurrent of resentment that colored the nation's feelings about so many stars. Moreover, they proved themselves adept at adjusting to the changing tides of that public's taste.

Fairbanks' first three United Artists releases were not substantially different from the work that had gone before. *His Majesty the American,* *When the Clouds Roll By,* and *The Mollycoddle* were relatively short modern comedies. It was his habit in these little films to take gentle satirical swipes at common social pretensions and fads, and in the few years of his heaviest production he had managed to comment on such diverse topics as hypochondria, Anglophilia, social-climbing by the new rich, success literature, the liberated woman (of whom bobbed hair was the symbol), patronizing social workers (a favorite theme of Griffith's, incidentally) as well as, in casual asides, such matters as modern dancing, Coueism, ouija boards, night-club entertainment, and so on. Alistair Cooke, who compiled this list, notes that the satire grew more obvious—though not less good-humored—as his career developed and he became "sure of his public and its trust in the essential health of his reaction to all affectation." In the first UA release he was seen as "an excitement-hunting thrill hound" bored by the constraints of life in narrow Manhattan. In the next he took on quack popular psychologizing, while in the last he was seen as an idle and fatuous English milord, that favorite figure of fun for the American democrat, though, of course, Fairbanks was careful to provide the character with ample opportunity to prove his fundamental worth by testing himself against the rigors of the American West and the inventive villainies of the heavies.

There was no falling off in the charm and humor of these pictures. On the other hand, there is reason to suppose that Fairbanks was beginning to be bored by the formula and that he sensed the public would soon be in a similar condition. Moreover, the general trend of the industry was against the modest film. *The Birth of a Nation* had started something that would not be stopped. Griffith's *Intolerance* had failed, to be sure, but De Mille's *Joan the Woman* had not and neither had Ince's *Civilization*. Even Griffith himself had made a partial recovery with his wartime *Hearts of the World* and his expensive *Way Down East* in 1920. It was perfectly clear that the public was intrigued by the cinema's unique ability to bring them drama on a scale the stage could not hope to duplicate, to transport them to realms the theater could not hope to capture realistically.

Nor was it merely the apparent limitlessness of the screen's scope that compelled movie-makers to broaden their canvases and encouraged the public to support their experiments. It is a cliché of social history to note that World War One produced an era of disillusionment among artists and intellectuals and a huge need for escapism among the masses. There are more exceptions to this generalization than it is entirely convenient to enumerate, but it is also largely true. There was a great outpouring of emotion over the selection and burial of an unknown soldier in Arlington National Cemetery in 1921, but this was a last gasp of populist sentiment for something like a decade. Neither in life nor the movies were people much interested in anonymous heroes claiming to represent the collective will. They wanted their heroic figures to be clearly defined, standing out colorfully against the grayness of the crowd. They preferred them to be, if anything, excessive in their romantic appeal, like Valentino, and they preferred to see them in settings that were as distant as possible in time or space from the American scene of the time. If the setting was to be American, the preferred milieu was upper class. De Mille had great success at the turn of the decade with his seemingly sophisticated studies of marital infidelities among the prosperous. Ordinary people struggling with the ordinary problems of day-to-day existence, the very stuff of the movies' first popular successes, were now out, and would not appear again—and then briefly—until that decade of the common man, the 1930s.

This generally expansive and escapist mood suited Fairbanks' own feelings perfectly. Indeed, according to his son, "The idea of making bigger and more spectacular films had been in the back of his mind for years." His favorite literary hero was D'Artagnan and he had tried out the character in his 1918 release, *A Modern Musketeer*. It was the story of a young Kansan fired into gallant comic orbit by his reading of the Dumas novel. He had included a brief dream sequence in which he could test himself in the D'Artagnan role and had been well pleased by the results. In the meantime, his friends and advisors kept suggesting dashing folk, historical and fairy-tale heroes that might suit him.

Finally, Ruth Allen, who had been a play agent, recommended that he read a book called *The Curse of Capistrano*, which was based on the true, if legend-encrusted, story of a hero of Spanish California history, Zorro, and Fairbanks decided it would be an excellent and not overly expensive means of testing public acceptance of him in a costume role. The settings were readily available—just outside his window, as it were—and they were not troublingly unfamiliar. After all, something like a decade's worth of Westerns had utilized them. In short, here was an opportunity to introduce a new character in a new context—the historical—that was minimally dislocating to Fairbanks' public. Moreover, that character itself—set aside costume and the rapier he so gracefully wielded—was not so very different from the ones the actor had been doing in modern dress. Zorro, of course, was an aristocrat who had placed his sword at the service of the common people. Caped and masked, he was unrecognizable to the blundering soldiery of the Spanish king. But to complete the disguise, and to create a deliciously comic contrast, his public persona was that of a witless and limp-wristed idler almost giddily effeminate in manner.

Fairbanks was by no means certain that this creation would be a success, so he produced it comparatively cheaply and, almost simultaneously did another—and, as it happened, the last—of his modern comedies. Called *The Nut*, it satirized social workers and was one of his few commercial failures. *Zorro*, of course, was a huge success and he almost immediately put the long-nourished *Three Musketeers* into production. It was ready for release less than a year after *Zorro* had been placed before the public, only six months after *The Nut* was released and, more elaborate than *Zorro*, it was an even greater success.

Robert E. Sherwood, a great Fairbanks enthusiast—he would later do one of the actor's lesser scripts—was then the movie reviewer for the old *Life* and he began his piece thus:

"When Alexandre Dumas sat down at his desk, smoothed his hair back, chewed the end of his quill pen, and said to himself, 'Well, I guess I might as well write a book called *The Three*

Musketeers, he doubtless had but one object in view: to provide a suitable story for Douglas Fairbanks to act in the movies."

Sherwood went on to call the film "marvelous" and to state that "never has a famous character from a famous novel found finer treatment in a movie. . . . Not only is the physical grace and superb poise there—but also the intense fire, the animation of spirit that was so vital a part of Dumas' magnificent hero." He noted, as did other critics, that playwright Edward Knoblock's adaptation of the novel was quite a free one. In particular it was observed that Constance, seamstress to the queen and D'Artagnan's true love, was no longer married to another man, was not characterized as the hero's mistress, and does not die at the end of the film as she did at the end of the book. There was also the occasional quibble that the Paris of the film looked "too neat and tidy, somewhat as though it were 'made in America' "—which, of course, it was.

Still, even the critics themselves admitted that these were the merest matters of detail and Sherwood ended his review by saying, "It takes rank with *The Four Horsemen of the Apocalypse* and *The Kid* as one of the great achievements of the movies." This was an odd bracketing, or so it seems from the vantage point of a half-century later—the former film was so pretentious and heavy, the latter so simple and affecting. The problem for Sherwood and for other early film critics who wanted to make the public take movies as seriously as they did, was somehow to communicate the sense that this was a work of quality, a thing that had elicited from its producer a high degree of careful craftsmanship and good taste, a sober respect for the screen's artistic potential, no matter how frivolous the film's source material.

This was something that Fairbanks, too, was concerned about, though he was modest enough about his own abilities as an actor in the conventional sense of the term. "He often said that Mary Pickford and I had genius," Chaplin reports, "while he had only a small talent." It seems that he wanted to exert himself as what would later be termed, somewhat derogatorily, a "creative producer" in order to compensate for the narrowness of his range. It is also possible to imagine that acting—a very sometime sort of occupation in the new age of the movies, when you might work once a year rather than once a week, as had been possible in the days of the one- and two-reeler, and where, of course, a long run was an impossibility—could not absorb his enormous energies. Anyway, he appears to have loved the process of mounting his increasingly elaborate films, absorbing himself in the million-and-one details of the work. It was man's work—business—in the age when business was said to be the business of America, and it appears to have greatly pleased him to set hundreds of craftsmen to work on projects that would, ultimately, employ similar numbers of players. This was success as "The Americano" truly understood it, with which he was truly comfortable. A reporter from *The New York Times* seems to have sensed the change that was coming over the actor as early as the New York premiere of *The Three Musketeers*, when he described him as "a slightly heavier Fairbanks, with a businessman's moustache, who took the stage to express his thanks" for the audience's approval of the film.

Around this time Chaplin recalls a warm summer's night when he and Fairbanks went out for a ramble through a Beverly Hills that was still a wilderness (Greyhall had been only the second house built there and it was not until Pickfair—another early building—was remodelled to Fairbanks' taste that the area became fashionable and, slightly later, populous). They decided to climb to the top of a water tank to gain a better view of both the night sky and the hills that sheltered the strolling players. The stars were brilliant, the moon "incandescent," as Chaplin remembered them, and he was encouraged to wax philosophical about the ironic contrast between such heavenly beauty and the meaninglessness of the scramble here below.

Fairbanks was having nothing of such gloom. "Look! The moon! And the myriads of stars!" he cried. "Surely there must be a reason for all this beauty? It must be fulfilling some destiny! It must be for some good and you and I are all a part of it!" Suddenly inspired, he turned to Chaplin and challenged him: "Why are you given this talent, this wonderful medium of motion pictures that reaches millions of people throughout the world?"

Fairbanks' romantic ebullience always brought out the cynic in Chaplin and he replied: "Why is it given to Louis B. Mayer and the Warner Brothers?" Fairbanks had the grace to laugh at his own excess, to see that there was no necessary correlation between artistic talent and economic reward. Still . . .

Yet he wanted to assert himself by making still more magnificent films, films on the grandest scale ever conceived. Knoblock had suggested he follow *Musketeers* with either *Ivanhoe* or *Robin Hood*, and both titles were submitted to the United Artists sales department in New York for a prediction about exhibitor reaction. Word came back that *Robin Hood* would likely be a better seller. Fairbanks instructed his staff to research the period, then took off for a European holiday where the idea germinated further. On his return, there was a heavy round of story conferences and, as was his well-organized habit, a chart, outlining the basic plot of the film, soon went up on his office wall. From this, according to Douglas, Jr., another chart, this time breaking the plot down into sequences, was made and, soon enough, a third chart, this one a scene-by-scene analysis, was created. From it, the scenario, which would bear his pseudonym (Elton Thomas), even though it could scarcely be called a single-handed creation, was eventually drawn.

In all, the creation of *Robin Hood* would consume something more than a year of his life and establish the pattern he would follow for the rest of the decade, in which each film would require a similar expenditure of time. *Robin Hood*, indeed, would rival, in the cost and magnificence of its setting—if not, surely, the complexity of its story line and theme—Griffith's *Intolerance*. Indeed, it's a nice question whether the Walls of Babylon which Griffith had caused to be run up for his 1915 masterpiece or the castle set for Fairbanks' production was the more lavish. It is written, however, that the latter covered some ten acres on the studio backlot and the whole enterprise was seen as "an act of bravado worthy of 'Doug' "—worthy, that is, of the bustling, optimistic young examplar of the American spirit of enterprise whom he was now phasing out as his screen persona. For something of an economic recession had gripped Hollywood at the time and the construction of this set, and the casting of enough extras to fill it with life, was, says Cooke, an attempt "to solve Hollywood's chronic unemployment problem." If not that, it was certainly a statement of confidence in the industry's future, a bold assertion of leadership when others were not in so forthcoming a mood.

Which is not to say that Fairbanks was entirely without moments of hesitation. His son asserts that throughout the preproduction stages of the film he was assailed by uncharacteristic doubts—about the scale of the enterprise he had undertaken and, therefore, about the details of the story line on which it was built.

He was not present, apparently, when his brother Robert, who was a trained engineer, began executing the designs of Wilfred

Buckland, a stage designer who had worked for that master of spectacular theatrical architecture, David Belasco. And when he saw what Robert had wrought, even dauntless Doug was somewhat daunted. He was, however, conducted on an inspection tour by the director, Allan Dwan (also an engineer by training), and Dwan carefully pointed out to him the well-placed handholds that would enable him to clamber the walls gracefully, the trampoline hidden behind the battlements that would enhance his leaps when he scampered along, the slide hidden behind the long draperies, a simple extension—to a height of several stories—of that commonest piece of playground equipment. When the inspection was completed, Fairbanks was entirely won over, and Dwan would later recall that he took an almost childish delight in conducting friends around the set, demonstrating the marvelous tricks he could do on it.

So proprietary was he, in fact, that his brother cheerfully went along with a splendid practical joke dreamed up by the best of those friends. Robert called Fairbanks one day, before *Robin Hood* had gone into production, to say that an independent producer wanted to rent the set for a day's shooting. Fairbanks, needless to say, was outraged. That glorious edifice was, next to his own name, likely to be the major attraction of the film, and he was not about to give the audience a preview of it. Still, his brother persisted. Wouldn't Fairbanks just come down to the lot and see what the man wanted to do? What could it cost him just to look?

All right, he'd look. When the appointed hour arrived, Robert Fairbanks conducted him to a spot in front of the great drawbridge and, in a moment, it began to creak down. There was a pause and then a tiny figure, clad in nightgown and cap, strolled across the bridge, yawned, placed an empty milk bottle and a kitten down on the ground and strolled back into the castle, the bridge creaking up behind him. The tiny figure, of course, was Chaplin, and Fairbanks who loved elaborate practical jokes as much as he loved elaborate productions, collapsed with laughter.

The film itself proved to be every bit as appealing as Chaplin's gag. Like most of Fairbanks' other big films of this decade, it was unmarred by straining for significance, by that desire to make some broadly significant cultural, historical, or literary statement that marked so many competing films. For all its length and splendor, it was what it was—just a movie. Vachel Lindsay thought that it was, perhaps, rather too rooted in one spot—that expensive castle—lacking the free movement through space that both *Zorro* and *The Three Musketeers* exhibited. The latter, especially, the poet had liked, "for the simple reason that a plot based on flight and pursuit down the highway, down the street, down the lane, and across the sea and back is essentially a photoplay resource"—which he argued was unduplicable in any other medium. *Robin Hood*, he felt, was duplicable, for wasn't that castle essentially just a giant stage set?

It is hard to argue with a writer whose instinctive understanding of the movieness of movies was so far in advance of his time, who was so determined to try to establish an esthetic for them that owed nothing to the other arts. Moreover, it is true that the film lacked the narrative flow of the other Fairbanks films. The problem, despite all Fairbanks' charts and planning, was structural. Most of the pomp and pageantry was in the first half, which revolved around the twelfth-century court life of the legendary Richard the Lion-Hearted as he prepared to leave for the Crusades—the venture that would cost him, so the story goes, years in prison, and place his evil brother, John, on the English throne. Though ravishing to look at, and genially accepted by the public, this section, in which

Fairbanks, occasionally weighed down by armor, appears as the Earl of Huntington, is ponderous in comparison to what people expected of him. Once the Earl takes his revolutionary stance, however, and organizes his band of Merrie Men and takes the name of the film's title character, the picture begins to right itself. Or, as one critic of the time put it, "Old England gets a thorough jazzing." Indeed, this anonymous reviewer—as opposed to later writers—was inclined to think it too bad—"considering the tremendous advance the first part of the picture makes over anything Fairbanks has done before"— that he chose a comic-opera style for the Sherwood Forest sections and that his own performance was throughout perhaps a little too self-consciously theatrical. The man from the *Times* disagreed. He, too, gave *Robin Hood* high marks for its settings and pageantry ("never . . . equalled before, surely never surpassed") but liked, as well, the "lively, loping story" that developed so rapidly in the second part through "a quick succession of starts and skirmishes and escapes, with Robin Hood darting and sending darts everywhere." It is here, he said, "that Douglas Fairbank · had his fun. And how those in the theater last night enjoyed him."

It was, then, a Janus-like film—looking backward to the Dashing Doug of the early films, forward to the Douglas Fairbanks to come, when the spectacular showman's side of his nature would be in the ascendant. In no other film would the conflict between these two aspects of his personality be so obvious, and so obviously unresolved. The public, however, either did not notice or did not care. *Robin Hood* represented the height of their love affair with him. At the New York premiere a special midnight screening had to be hastily scheduled to accommodate the throng that could not find seats for the great event itself and could not be persuaded to leave the sidewalk in front of the Lyric Theater and come back another day. In the year when Griffith failed dismally with another melodramatic spectacle, *Orphans of the Storm*, when von Stroheim scandalized moralists with his wickedly satirical—and amusingly self-satirizing—*Foolish Wives* and the intellectual community was much bemused by the potential of a new film form called the documentary—exemplified by *Nanook of the North—Robin Hood* was surely the box-office success of the year.

And, for better or for worse, it did assert Fairbanks' claim to leadership in Hollywood, for the next year was rich in spectacle. De Mille abandoned upper-class sin as a subject and got religion in spectacular fashion by producing *The Ten Commandments*. Lon Chaney's *The Hunchback of Notre Dame*, with its boiling mobs and its great cathedral set, was in its way as stupendous as anything Fairbanks ever attempted. Even the Western, that low-budget staple, was dressed out in new and expensive finery and—although austere Bill Hart would have nothing to do with such fripperies, turning down the proffered lead, as well as the chance for a comeback—James Cruze's *The Covered Wagon* was an enormous hit in 1923.

IX

But Fairbanks himself was not yet finished with spectacle. He passed 1923, which also happened to be the year of his fortieth birthday, working on the most ambitious and, as it turned out, the most critically controversial, of his films—*The Thief of Bagdad*.

Most recent commentators have followed the line suggested by Cooke, that he was here attempting "to better the example of the German historical costume film (*Passion, All for a Woman, Gypsy Blood*)" then enjoying an international vogue. In the end, according to Cooke, the film, "made at prodigious cost," succeeded only in suffocating "the old beloved sprite in a mess of décor." Alexander Walker adds that in *Thief*, as well as in the other films of the Twenties, "The armies of period historians, costume designers, special-effects men, and art directors . . . do not support their leader so much as swamp him . . . Where once he danced on air, Doug now stands on ceremony." And, writing at the time, Paul Rotha claimed that it was in his wish to encourage the "art" of the cinema "that Fairbanks strikes the wrong note. His most recent films have not had the rough power, the intensity, or the vigor" of the earlier, less-pretentious works.

There was some truth in this. And the theory behind it was well put by Cooke. "Even professional gymnasts need apparatus and are clannishly leery of uncertified ropes and fences and invitations to perform without well-resined hands. Fairbanks' glory, the mystery of his visual fascination, is that he could throw all the textbook tricks on the makeshift apparatus of ordinary life."

It was, he said, in the "virtuoso use of the landscape as a natural gymnasium whose equipment is invisible to the ordinary man, the use of his own body as a crazy but disciplined bow on something that turns into a handy fiddle, that made him an enchanting image . . ."

Cooke, of course, gives full marks to the quality of the gymnastics Fairbanks performed in the costume pictures, but the implication of his argument is obvious. These settings, however "accurate" they were in the historical sense, could not help but be stylizations. Moreover, they were extraordinary, even exotic stylizations. We expect something wondrous to occur in such contexts, and would be quite let down if it didn't happen. But in employing them he lost the value of contrast between his own unique gifts and the dull, normal world he had, in his earlier films, seemed to share with us.

Walker contrasts Fairbanks' work on the castle walls of *Robin Hood* and the even more stylized fairy-tale city of *Thief* with a simple little sequence in one of the earlier films. In it, he played a character convinced that it was bad luck to permit a black cat to cross his path. To avoid one he clambered gracefully up a drainpipe, did a simple flip onto—and then off of—a balcony, without ruffling either his impeccable suit or his comic dignity—and without losing his black homburg. One must admit that the simple charm and sheer inventiveness of the modern-dress trick was singularly engaging—and its gentle satire on the lengths people will go to serve their superstitions was perhaps more resonant than anything in the costume pictures.

There were other defects in these later films. Sometimes it seemed that things, inanimate objects, now dominated Fairbanks and that he had lost his ability to dominate them, as he had in the beginning. Sometimes, too, his confidence seemed to deteriorate into braggadocio and narcissism, and the cruel element, always present in physical comedy, whether it be practiced by Chaplin or Mickey Mouse, sometimes became too obvious, as, increasingly, Fairbanks used people rather thoughtlessly—playing casually off their weaknesses to make himself look good. Finally, all too often he cast himself as that creature he both envied and wished to emulate—the nobleman. To be sure, his sword was always placed in the service of the people, of democratic ideals, but it is also true that there was a touch of *noblesse oblige,* hence of condescension, in the costume roles. Indeed, of the late films, it was only in *The Thief of Bagdad* that he played a commoner, and then in a context so odd that it was difficult to draw analogies between Fairbanks and any reality the audience knew or felt.

On the other hand, there were values in these later films—especially in *The Thief of Bagdad*—that have been insufficiently stressed by later commentators. It may be, as Cooke and others have suggested, that the impressive German spectacle films, with their self-conscious ambition to blend the values of the modernist tradition in the plastic and architectural arts, with a narrative tradition borrowed from folk material, influenced Fairbanks. Indeed, they influenced nearly everyone involved in film production at the time—including even such an unlikely figure as the young Alfred Hitchcock, just beginning his career as a director. Nevertheless, Fairbanks, though "impressed by the better German films . . . did not like them as commercial enterprises and usually opposed suggestions that United Artists distribute them," according to his son. He sought always—if not always successfully—to infuse his films with the basic values of the *American* film—action and humor and a certain light, self-mocking irony. It is certainly there, if you look for it, in *Thief.* Moreover, that film had no precedent and precious few successors in American film history. The marvelously stylized Arabian nights settings, built on the foundations of the great *Robin Hood* set, to this day strike the eye as fresh, original—and suggest paths still not fully explored by film-makers. Similarly, the special effects—Doug on his flying carpet, Doug flinging skyward a magical rope that stiffened so he could climb it, Doug battling sundry fantastic monsters in a series of tests he must pass before claiming his Princess' hand—are technically adroit and charming fun.

Fairbanks the producer had never been more imaginative or inventive. Or serious. He had originally engaged Maxfield Parrish, the great illustrator, to design the film, though all he retained of his work was the marvelous poster he did for the advertising campaign—perhaps the most beautiful such object ever created. He tried a couple of replacements, searching for the man who could translate his magical vision into concrete terms, before settling on the youthful, gifted William Cameron Menzies, who turned out to have no peer in this realm of movie and theatrical design (among his later credits were *Gone with the Wind* and *Around the World in 80 Days*, both instances in which his contributions turned out to be the most distinguished things about the productions).

In short, it was a notable, daring, and worthwhile experiment in film-making, an attempt to expand the bounds of the spectacle film, and it was much appreciated at the time. The early film historian, Benjamin Hampton, considered *The Thief of Bagdad* (along with *Ben Hur* and *King of Kings*) as "noteworthy achievements of the American civilization which inspired them." Robert Sherwood commented: "I now know what it means to be able to say, 'Well, I've been to the top.'" More important, he singled out the quality that gives this picture, so grievously abused by later critics, its special appeal when he wrote: "Fairbanks has gone far beyond the mere bounds of possibility; he has performed the superhuman feat of making his magic seem probable."

Vachel Lindsay went even further. He was, he said, an advocate of seeing particularly worthwhile films at least ten times and he found *The Thief of Bagdad* eminently worthy of such extensive study. He proposed seeing it three times "just to enjoy the story and the splendor," a couple of times "for reminiscences of Griffith's magnificent *Intolerance*," another time to observe how Fairbanks had digested both "the glories and the mistakes of *Intolerance*." (The director, the engaging Raoul Walsh, was scarcely ever mentioned in reviews of the film, and neither were his colleagues, who worked on other Fairbanks films, so obviously was the actor the "auteur" of his movies.) In addition, the poet felt one should devote at least one screening to "watching that great actor of which until now you have been unconscious, the sea." It was, he added, "the first actor in the movies, and the last. Into it dives the hero, on it rides the magic boat. The sea is the greatest actor of both *The Thief of Bagdad* and *The Black Pirate*."

But the heart of his appreciation—three showings—lay in the fact that *Thief* so beautifully illustrated two values that lay at the center of his eccentric, yet somehow persuasive, film esthetic—"architecture in motion" and "sculpture-in-motion." "You can spend one whole evening just watching stairways and see how they leap like race horses from scene to scene, or pour like cataracts through the various archways." They were, these stairways, "actors in the grand manner," to Lindsay's eyes. As for the sculptural aspect of the film, he cried: "See how the sentinels and combatants when close to the camera are gigantic bronzed figures much larger than life and carved as by a living chisel. You utterly forget how large they are until you compare them with the face of the clock by the side of the stage." Conversely, he asks us to "notice how the hand of prince or princess can be big as the whole screen without in any way being inelegant or silly, but seemingly as delicate as the hand of Tom Thumb's wife."

We tend now to take all this for granted. In fact, the sound film so firmly directed our attention toward narrative, away from plastic values, that we forget that the silent film, by choice and by necessity, had sometimes to stress these values in order to hold our attention—or merely to dazzle it just for the fun, the showmanship, of it. But Lindsay is right. These values are dominant in *Thief* and, given a story that is "sound and workable" in Sherwood's words, one that "proceeds rhythmically and gracefully at a steadily increasing rate of speed," it seems wrong-headed of later critics to be at such pains to reverse the contemporary judgment of the film. To be sure, its moral, oft-repeated in subtitles, that "happiness must be earned" is rather thin. To be sure, here as elsewhere in his later films, Fairbanks seems to be uncomfortably forcing himself beyond his natural limits as an actor and thus encouraging a reliance on rather stagey mannerisms that, admittedly, suffered in contrast to his old ease and naturalism. But if some of what was best in the old Doug was lost beyond recall, he was obviously doing his best to compensate for its absence and, it should be firmly recorded, these compensations wear very well. The wit, gaiety, and inventiveness that went into his *mise-en-scene* still delight us a half-century later, still attest to the film-maker's integrity and respect for his audience—qualities that would later be less in evidence in his work.

The Thief of Bagdad was in no sense the creation of a man over-confident of his audience's affection, lazily trading on his reputation. Manifestly, he worked hard and took that work with great seriousness. He was giving good value to his customers.

Yet one speaks here with a certain false objectivity—as one who was not part of the generation that "discovered" Fairbanks and had a proprietary interest in his career because initially his screen character reflected back at it some part of its own spirit, its sense of self. Most of the generation, grateful for past pleasures, was willing to concede him the right to try anything he wanted. After all, they were his contemporaries and understood that the interests of a successful man in his forties might well be different from those of a striving man in his thirties. Their loyalty, demonstrated in writing like Lindsay's, was uncritical and unswerving. And, on balance, I think Lindsay was closer to the mark critically about the late films than Cooke was. Taken on their own terms, considered as objects isolated from the drama of Fairbanks' own career, they are never less than interesting, often important, works.

X

But the critics had a point that is incorrectly made in purely esthetic terms. They sensed that somehow the artist, and the man, was heading in a direction that was wrong for him, even dangerous.

They valued him as an artist more highly than he himself did. They found his ambitions as producer, celebrity, would-be leader of his art-*cum*-industry unseemly. There was no precedent for such ambitions in the other arts and there was an ideal model available in this art—Chaplin's. Like Fairbanks, he functioned as his own producer and writer (and director too), but he placed these gifts in the service of a much more austere and traditional calling—self-expression, as it has been customarily defined in the arts. Deliberately restricting himself to his "Little Fellow" characterization, experimenting not at all with technique, making no attempt to charm the public when he was off-screen (quite the opposite, in fact), keeping very much to himself in Hollywood, he established a standard of apparent integrity compared to which any other mode of celebrity behavior was bound to seem rather showy.

Partly this was a matter of temperament. Chaplin said recently: "I didn't know many actors in California. I was mostly alone there. It was always hard to make friends. I was shy and inarticulate. Doug Fairbanks was my only real friend and I was a showpiece for him at parties." Partly, it was a matter of ambition. Chaplin craved the admiration and the company of the intellectual community while Fairbanks went after the society crowd. The result—an undervaluation of Fairbanks—drove Vachel Lindsay crazy: "The people who are completely hoity-toity and perish at the thought of agreeing with the majority finally decided, after your humble servant dingdonged at them for years, that it was time to look around and patronize at least one movie person and not be contaminated by the rest. Writers whom I will not mention have learned to speak the name of Charlie Chaplin with a sigh . . . and then have no more to do with the movies." They would not accept the notion that Fairbanks was also an artist and a leader. Nor would they accept the notion, implicit in Lindsay's argument, that in a communal and industrially based art, the very term "artist" perhaps required redefinition, or at least expansion. Indeed, Lindsay claimed that it was Fairbanks who started the whole Chaplin cult. "Whenever anybody that looks like a painful highbrow gets within ten feet of Fairbanks, he begins to tell him how Charlie Chaplin is the next thing to Whistler. Sometimes he compares him to one of the Barrymores. He compares him to anything that shows that Charlie is in a class all by himself." Partly it was a matter of philosophy. Chaplin was not as deep as his admirers believe him to have been. But there is no question that his "Little Fellow" was an attempt to make some sort of Universal Statement about the Human Condition. About that matter, Fairbanks had nothing to say. He was an American and, as such, didn't think much about the big questions. He could cheerfully, unmaliciously, satirize the fads and foibles of the moment—as he had in his early pictures—but especially at the height of his powers, when everything seemed to be going so well for him and for a prospering nation, he would not distance himself from the optimistic values of his society. How could he? Hadn't everything worked out nicely for him? Wasn't he living proof that the spirit of Horatio Alger still moved in the land? Wasn't he rich and famous and well-married and in charge of his own destiny? Wasn't he, for all that, freer in some ways even than a captain of industry chained to his desk, unable to move about in the world, surround himself with handsome, elegant, well-born, high-achieving people?

But that, precisely, is what Cooke and the other critics were driving at. The late films were beautiful to look at, full of thrills and fun and difficult technical problems solved in exemplary fashion. What was missing from them was not humanity—they thronged with that—but human-ness. The pleasures Lindsay, for example, enumerated were largely abstract ones. Staircases and the sea were listed as great actors, but Douglas Fairbanks was not. Even Lindsay had to admit that "on points" Chaplin, perhaps even Valentino, could "beat" Fairbanks as an actor. The thing was that "there is no leadership in Rudolph. There is no leadership in Chaplin, no particular sense of being a public citizen after the fashion, we will say, of Roosevelt in his boyish days."

The poet did not, perhaps in those days could not, be expected to understand the full implications of what he was saying—any more than Fairbanks could be expected to apprehend the full implications of what he was doing and what was being done to him. After a half century or so of living with the celebrity system, perhaps we can do a little better. Surely we understand that the minute anyone becomes a "leader"—artistic, intellectual, political— he begins to lose touch with his audience, his constituency. At the same time he begins to lose touch with himself, that is, with those instinctive understandings of issues—psychological, moral, social, whatever—that he once unselfconsciously encapsulated, then articulated, thereby building his first fame.

The process is almost automatic. These people are endowed, it seems, with some sort of magic. They seem so effortlessly to create, out of themselves, metaphors of understanding, organizing for us inchoate but recognizable ideas and emotions and then showing us how to deal with them—earnestly or gracefully or stylishly or angrily, whatever seems appropriate. The point is that they are enough like us so that we quite naturally want to reach out and touch them and, to a point, they are required to let us do so—making themselves available for interviews, personal appearances, and, lately of course, to the television cameras.

On the other hand, they are different from us precisely to the degree that they have had the talent (in combination with greater or lesser degrees of luck) to perform the organizing and projective tasks to which we have responded and to the degree that by so doing they achieve a distancing wealth and fame. In addition, of course, they have an understandable human need for privacy and to assert their difference from the crowd. In time they must come to loathe that portion of the audience that wishes to fawn on them, while fearing that psychopathic minority that envies them so much that it wishes to harm them. Wealth, of course, buys them walls and retreats. It also permits the growth of an ever-increasing entourage that moves protectively with their principal along the ever-more-circumscribed circle of places where they may safely allow themselves to be seen. At this point in a public career, obviously, the celebrity's access to material with which he might broaden, deepen, or refresh his ideas or his art, is profoundly narrowed. And that point generally coincides with that moment when he has drained his original pool of inspiration dry, when he most desperately needs to be open to the world, free to let his imagination roam across it.

At this moment many self-destruct—especially those who owe their success more to luck than to talent. We nowadays see on the television talk shows how those who survive attempt to live off themselves—and, as a result, often starve to death before our very eyes. In all the varieties of celebrity behavior there is an element of self-parody. Sometimes that's all there is, as in the case of actors who permit what might once have been the elements of a style to deteriorate into a collection of consumer-tested mannerisms—Steve McQueen's spoiled-child poutings, Paul Newman's eternal boyishness. Still others, especially comedians, attempt to demonstrate the sobriety of their humanitarian and artistic concerns—Danny Kaye and Jerry Lewis, respectively and boringly.

Then there are the players who seek new worlds to conquer and we witness such unlikely transformations as Shirley MacLaine the political pundit, Jane Fonda the political activist. Conversely, literary men, juiced on celebrity, become role players, creating actorish public personalities in the manner of Norman Mailer, who remains the most engaging of the lot because he actually seems to know what he's doing, communicating a certain ironic and energetic joy in his put-on. The most absurd of them—the Marshall McLuhans and the Buckminster Fullers—become oracular and gnomic gurus, cult figures expanding an original and limited web of ideas until it breaks and scatters in nonsensical fragments. But perhaps the worst and most dangerous effect of converting all of public life into a celebrity playground occurs in the political realm.

Witness the Kennedy phenomenon, in which for the first time a Presidency was maintained almost solely on the basis of a glamorous and enviable life style—the movie-fan magazines took to covering the doings of the White House family as if it were located in Beverly Hills—and perhaps destroyed by a psychopath enraged at the contrast between that life style and his own. Or consider the 1972 Presidential election, in which the personally dreary winner—often a loser because he could not handle the elements of modern celebrityhood—refused to play the game under its new rules, and crudely but effectively manipulated the media by alternately intimidating and hiding from it, while the loser, imprisoned by an entourage of idealogues, found it impossible to establish communication with a broad constituency, demonstrating not the slightest awareness of what was on their minds. At one level, the campaign came down to a contest between a man who ostentatiously, moralistically turned his back on the celebrity system—using its own technology to communicate that message—and one who embraced it without being fully aware of its great danger, its capacity to alienate and delude its would-be manager.

It is at once amusing and terrifying to observe that after more than five decades of living with the celebrity system, seeing how it works and how it has affected the lives of their predecessors, the people whose careers depend on a sophisticated understanding of its workings are strangely innocent about it. It was fair enough, early in the game, for Fairbanks to resent having to worry about how the public would respond to his marriage to Mary Pickford. Their situation was truly without precedent. At this late date, however, there is something ludicrous about a star's resentment of the public's intrusive interest in his private life and beliefs, his insistence that all he owes to his public are good performances. It is now a fact established for over a half-century, a fact that ought to be well known to any actor entering the movies and aspiring some day to see his name above some film's title, that the system will exact from him the tribute of lost privacy in return for found prosperity—and that it is useless, and at least as wearing, to resist its functioning as it is to go along with it. The same stricture holds true, of course, to everyone else in public life today, the movie-star model now applying to every aspect of that life. All of which is a way of saying that the case of Fairbanks, as one of the earliest and most exuberant members of this new realm of power in America, elicits more sympathy than most. Nowadays, at least, the practical matters of managing a career at the top are quite easily taken care of. There is a well-articulated structure designed to serve those who suffer the accident of stardom—agents, accountants, lawyers, public relations advisors (some of whom are actually competent)—and the possibility of emerging more or less intact from the ordeal of superstardom is a reasonable one. But Fairbanks, Pickford, and their peers had to begin the creation of that system under the pressure of coping with fast-moving, unpredictable careers. Whatever one thinks of the way they handled the task, it must be seen against the perspective of the literally unimaginable difficulties they faced. For Fairbanks and the rest, the end was necessarily unknown and unknowable, and one feels the shock of his bewilderment when things started to go badly for him. He had, it seems, a right to a happier ending, given the cheerful energy and the basically optimistic spirit he brought to his pioneering in this new realm of the American experience, the liveliness of his interest in the new areas his sudden wealth and fame opened up to him, and the attractive innocence about the way he tried to handle himself during these good, rich years.

XI

How sweet it must have been, this life that seemed enviable enough at the time and grows even more so in retrospect. The center of it was, of course, Pickfair, which Fairbanks had acquired before he acquired his second wife. "Pickfair . . . could never be truly regarded as being extravagant in its architecture," Douglas Fairbanks, Jr., has commented, adding that "there are actually quite a few other houses which are considerably larger and more extravagant." Still, as redesigned by architect Wallace Neff in what the younger Fairbanks satirically refers to as "Semi-Colonial-Georgian" style, it was entirely suitable for the newlyweds. It did not overawe; it rambled comfortably. Conservatively and tastefully furnished in a manner photographs suggest was influenced perhaps by the country seats of the English nobility, the walls gradually filling with Fairbanks' collection of Western art and the paintings and objects he gathered on his foreign travels. Its greatest appeal was its site—high on a hill, "surrounded by vast gardens and wooded sections," most of sprawling, growing Los Angeles in sight, the circle of peasant homes in Beverly Hills growing closer and closer, as if seeking the protection of the Lord and Lady of the Manor.

They, in their turn, lived with a certain serenity behind the high stucco walls. On those rare occasions when they were not entertaining or going out—they always let it quietly be known that they preferred to be seated together at dinner parties—simplicity was the keynote at Pickfair. They might, for example, pass the evening screening a new movie, chewing peanut brittle as the action proceeded. Similarly, an ordinary day might begin with Fairbanks doing a prebreakfast jog about the grounds, after which his wife would appear in his dressing room to help him select, from his forty or so suits and his dozens of shirts and ties, his apparel for the day, though both knew that when he arrived at the studio he would shuck this finery in favor of flannels and a sweater or polo shirt.

This working garb was no affectation. He exercised in his gym every day and generally more than once a day. And then, of course, there were skills and stunts for his films that had to be perfected—sometimes over periods of weeks and even months. He had arrived in Hollywood a superb rider and all-around gymnast, and a quite competent fencer. This last skill he honed to world-class quality—we have the testimony of his coach on this point—for *The Three Musketeers*, and he kept it up. For the same film he perfected a single-handed handspring (the other hand, of course, held a sword at the ready). For *Robin Hood* he learned to use a spear—he practiced with a tent pole—as a vaulting pole. For the rather modest and engaging *Don Q, Son of Zorro*, sequel to *The Mark of Zorro* and immediate successor to *The Thief of Bagdad*, he became an adept with the Australian stock whip, which was first cousin to the American bullwhip. His biographers give an astonishing list of the tricks he accomplished with it in the film: he disarmed an enemy swordsman, put out a lighted candle, cut in two the contract for a forced marriage, broke a bottle, captured a wild bull, snapped a cigarette out of the villain's mouth, brought down and tied up with it "a man of high rank and low morals," used it as a swing to mount a dungeon's walls, and make good his escape from the heavy's clutches. It required no less than six weeks' constant work to perfect these skills, scarcely less time to learn to throw the bola, the weighted rope that is the Argentine equivalent of our lasso, for *The Gaucho*.

In short, even without the distractions of his career as a producer and even without his hugely busy public and social life Fairbanks kept busy, and engagingly so—one of the lucky handful who, at least for a time, managed to make a seamless join between work and play. Indeed, for a while in the Twenties every aspect of his career fed and stimulated every other aspect of it.

Set aside, for the moment, the history of Fairbanks' career as an artist and consider in general terms the social history of the movies and the social history of "society"—that is, of the group that has passed for an élite based on birth and wealth in the United States. Both underwent a profound change during the Twenties, and those changes affected and were affected by Douglas Fairbanks and his wife.

In the beginning, when D. W. Griffith undertook the slow process of making them artistically (and then socially) respectable, the movies had been regarded as an extremely raffish outpost of show business and, of course, they were well beyond the pale as far as society—or, for that matter, the middle class—was concerned. Out-of-work legitimate actors literally sneaked into Griffith's Biograph studio when they were forced to take employment there in order to keep eating. Confident that their colleagues would never see them on the contemptible screen, they nevertheless worried that their shame might be glimpsed from the street, since The Biograph was located on 14th Street, then New York's busiest theatrical thoroughfare. Once inside, they discovered that many of their colleagues had had no previous connection whatever with the theater. Mack Sennett, for example, had been a steam-fitter; another comedy player, a trolley-car conductor; the prop boy, the call boy, and the chief cutter had been recruited from a neighborhood school. When the company went west in search of the sun each winter, it picked up cowboys and other drifting day laborers by the dozen. And what was true of Biograph was true of all the other movie companies. It was largely from these strong, essentially unlettered men, entirely unhampered by the traditions of high culture, let alone high society, that the first generation or two of American directors—who established the action melodrama and the knockabout comedy as our basic screen forms—was drawn. Their vigor and directness, not to mention their ability to stay effortlessly in touch with the common concerns of their audience, did much for the developing art of the film, but very little for its reputation in respectable circles. Then, of course, the fact that economically the movies came increasingly to be controlled by immigrants and the sons of immigrants—and mostly Jewish ones at that—did even less to enhance the reputability of the medium. It can, I think, be argued that much of the condescension with which the movies have been treated until very recently has its root in social rather than artistic snobbery.

Which is to say that the movies needed an opening to the East and that Fairbanks, with the contacts he had made in the Eastern social establishment during his Broadway days, with a life style based on the models he had studied at that time, was the perfect, even necessary figure to accomplish that. Indeed, though the formation of United Artists had elicited the oft-quoted industry gag about the lunatics taking over the asylum, the existence of the company was a vital, if inestimable, factor in creating new respect for the medium. The sight of Fairbanks moving easily in the most enviable circles not only represented a pleasing culmination to an aspect of the American dream; it also reassured the middle classes that the best people accepted at least some movie people as their equals. The presence of Mary Pickford, so demure and respectable, in the company's boardroom was also reassuring, a sign that, in a Hollywood increasingly bemused by subjects that seemed scandalous to her audience, someone would speak for (and produce films under the guidance of) traditional moral standards. Chaplin and even Griffith, whose work was declining in popularity during this period, served as earnests of serious artistic aspirations. In an industry with a not unjustified reputation for keeping an eye on the main chance, United Artists seemed a bastion of good taste and high aspirations. If it had produced nothing, it would have been a public-relations device of incalculable value.

But, of course, the residents of Pickfair didn't stop there. Richard Griffith has gone so far as to call them, "in all but name, unelected officials of the U.S. government," ever willing to lend their names to good causes, cheerfully traveling the length and breadth of the land to do their bit for their industry, their nation, the common good. As a pleasantly wicked contemporary journalist, Allene Talmey, put it at the time they provided "the necessary air of dignity, sobriety, and aristocracy. Gravely they attend movie openings, cornerstone layings, gravely sit at the head of the table at the long dinners in honor of the cinema great, Douglas making graceful speeches, Mary conducting herself with the self-abnegation of Queen Mary of Britain . . . they understand thoroughly their obligation to be present, in the best interests of the motion picture industry." This is not to say that Fairbanks became particularly stuffy or self-important. He was still capable of sweeping Mary up to a perch on his shoulder and carrying her thus down the aisle at one of his premieres. And of repairing to a New York rooftop, with press photographers in attendance, to pose with a bow and arrow to promote *Robin Hood*. "But," as Allan Dwan recalled it, "some deviltry within him made him let go of the arrow and away it flew"—across a street or two and through the open window of a loft where an immigrant tailor was sewing buttonholes. The missile lodged in the man's backside and he thought "that the American Indians were in revolt." He ran yelping into the street, where a policeman came to his aid and took him to Bellevue.

The incident cost Fairbanks $5,000 to settle amicably, but he was never cheap about anything, and when it came to publicity he was both a free and an imaginative spender. He was never more so than on the occasion of the New York premiere of *The Thief of Bagdad*, where the usherettes were dressed in harem costumes, allegedly Arabian perfumes were wafted through the auditorium, and Arabian coffee was served in the lobby. No doubt about it—he was temperamentally suited for the so-called "era of wonderful nonsense," nonsense generated, of course, by the emergence of the mass media as a genuine power in American life and by the rise of a powerful new industry—public relations—designed specifically to manipulate that force, to create for it what Boorstin would call "pseudo-events"—that is, happenings that had no function other than to provide the media with something to cover.

But the occasional publicity stunts were not the source of the hold Fairbanks and his wife held on their public or on our historical imaginations. For that matter, the success of their films does not suffice to explain it—plenty of stars made plenty of films that equaled theirs in popularity. No, there was something more here. In the Twenties, C. Wright Mills once explained, "socialities became really bored with Newport, and began to look to Broadway, then to Hollywood, for livelier playmates and wittier companions." Moreover, there emerged, just at this moment, thanks to prohibition, a place where "the institutional élite, the metropolitan socialite, and the professional entertainer" could mingle, "cashing in on one another's prestige." * That place, of course, was what came to be known as "café society"—a pleasant term for a group of speakeasies in New York that catered to this crowd, offering them, besides bootleg booze, the kind of protection from the common herd (who, of course, had an equal need of—and right to—the basic commodity purveyed in these places). There people, who might not visit one another's homes, could mingle in public, breaking down the old class lines. As Mills observed, John L. Sullivan could not be recognized by Mrs. Astor's Ward McAllister (inventor of the "400"), but Gene Tunney "was welcomed by café society." Where such a heady mixture of the truly accomplished and the merely wealthy, the merely well-bred and the merely notorious was to be found, the press was sure to follow—especially the new journalists of that day, the columnists and the reporters for the tabloids.

This is not to imply that Doug and Mary were regular members of café society. Far from it. It is to suggest that a major upheaval had occurred in the upper levels of American life and that Doug and Mary were the beneficiaries of it. Café society, which is actually a poor name for the embryo of the present-day celebrity system, was not, as Mills implies, confined to a few speakeasies in

---

* *Mills neglected to mention the professional criminals, but they were there, too, adding a whiff of danger to life at the top.*

Manhattan. If you were of it, you could find it everywhere. For soon enough, its members *did* begin to visit one another's homes and those homes turned out to be in all the right places, among them the places now associated with F. Scott Fitzgerald's life and work—for example, the Hamptons, the South of France, Paris. In fact, it begins to seem no accident that Fitzgerald ended up in Hollywood, trying to join a society that was, in so many respects, like the one he had known in his golden days. For Hollywood was rich enough—thanks not to inherited wealth, but to the fact that in the late Thirties it (unlike most American industries) was creating vast amounts of new wealth by cranking out a product for which people had an especially desperate need in that period—to remain insulated, essentially untouched by the depression.

Moreover, it retained the tone that Fairbanks had been instrumental in setting. That is, it was open to any interesting person who sought admission, but socially punishing to him if some misstep revealed the newcomer to be unworthy.* Finally, as Fitzgerald himself noted, movie-making has "a private grammar, like politics or automobile production or *society*" (emphasis added), and Beverly Hills is physically like the other playgrounds he and his fellows had previously known—warm, exotic in its foliage, heavily charged with sexual activity, providing ready access to amusing pastimes ranging from the familiar (tennis and golf) to the exotic (polo at the Will Rogers ranch, serious croquet on Darryl Zanuck's lawn), the whole environment conditioned by those big casinos where the fantasy life and work life of very beautiful and very rich people centered—the studios, where an endless, all-ab-

---

* For a harrowing account of the outlander overstepping the community's bounds and the panic—and punishment—resulting therefrom, see Fitzgerald's famous story "Crazy Sunday."

sorbing, high-stakes crap game was ever in progress. It was—and is—a place where action is everything, the winning and the losing less significant than being permitted to continue in the game and therefore in the life of the society around it, a place where the quality of the resulting product—the films themselves—was incidental, as unimportant in the larger sense as any other game in which the wealthy indulged.

Whatever you call it—society, café society, the celebrity system—it required a suitable embassy in Beverly Hills, a permanent legation, and it is precisely that which tasteful Pickfair and its tasteful owners provided. Before them, an expedition westward would have been quite unthinkable, the reception of emissaries from the far coast not something one could comfortably manage. Walter Wanger, one of the few Ivy Leaguers to know Hollywood in its very early days, claimed—just before he died—that Mack Sennett had been the social arbiter before Fairbanks and he summed up that producer's social style in a single succinct sentence: "If you didn't take the young lady on your right upstairs between the soup and the entrée, you were considered a homosexual." At least two serious scandals emanated from the Sennett circle—the death of Virginia Rappe during an orgy involving Fatty Arbuckle and the murder of a director and probable dope dealer named William Desmond Taylor in which comedienne Mabel Normand was implicated.* Quite obviously something a little finer was required, "the first organized social system" as Wanger identified the structure Doug and Mary created.

---

* One gets some idea of the tension that existed between this more raffish crowd and the emerging social order ruled over by the Fairbankses in a remark Miss Normand once made to a journalist: "Say anything you like, but don't say I like to work. That sounds too much like Mary Pickford, that prissy bitch." Miss Normand had begun under Griffith at Biograph, too, and she obviously found her one-time co-worker's social and artistic pretensions too much to bear.

The Fairbankses' reign was not unchallenged. Cecil B. De Mille was powerful, famous, a WASP—and he had his influence. Stars like Gloria Swanson, Pola Negri, and Mae Murray at one time or another found minor nobility to marry and were thereby able to burn brightly and briefly on the social scene. But though the public was fascinated by such goings-on, the fact remained that to traditional society and just plain newspaper readers, the life of "the movie colony" was mostly seen as one of wretched excess. It was Tom Mix spelling his name in huge electric lights on the roof of his home or arriving at the wedding of Rod La Rocque and Vilma Banky in a coach and four. It was Valentino's home being called "Falcon's Lair" and the star himself wearing a slave bracelet presented by his wife. It was Samuel Goldwyn's malapropisms, the ostentatious vulgarity of homes and cars and clothes of people as suddenly rich as the proprietors of a gold strike and about as careful with their winnings. It was a sense, above all, that the handful of well-publicized scandals of the Twenties represented merely the tip of the iceberg, that in an industry where sexual desirability was widely if often erroneously assumed to be the basis for a performer's success, a great deal more must be going on that we didn't know about, but were pleased to lasciviously speculate upon.

From all of that, Pickfair remained isolated. It wore its wealth easily, quietly, just as if it had been present for generations. And the fact that Fairbanks and Pickford were careful to create identities for themselves as something more than mere actors, were spokesmen-statesmen for their entire industry, was the most significant factor in differentiating them from the rest of the crowd. "When they were the social leaders, Pickfair was the pinnacle," said Walter Wanger. "To be invited to Pickfair was tops. Fairbanks and Pickford had toured the world. They had friends all over who came out to the estate." More of them, perhaps, than they wanted. Says Douglas Fairbanks, Jr.: "Many of the VIPs and visitors to Pickfair and the studio . . . tended to propose themselves . . . letters and telegrams would come from friends introducing other friends who were coming to California and asking if my father and Mary would ask them around or put them up. This often led to some curious mixtures—as you can imagine."

There was always an undercurrent of envious Hollywood gossip about Pickfair. "Doug goes to Europe each year to book his royal visitors for the coming year," one local wit claimed. And they liked to tell the apocryphal story about a Princess Vera Romanoff arriving in town, a car mysteriously arriving from Pickfair to transport her there for a party-filled weekend. "She was actually a little secretary from San Francisco," according to Wanger, "who went back on Monday morning, having thanked them very much." The younger Fairbanks doubts the validity of the story, though he concedes that "similar things" may have occurred in the rich, full life of Pickfair.

The gossip, however, was wrong. "I was simply a young man typical of my age," Evelyn Waugh wrote of this time. "We traveled as a matter of course." Fairbanks understood that fact of upper-class life even if the provincials of Hollywood did not. And as his son was later to write: "It was never really necessary for them, or indeed for most celebrities, to seek out people from worlds other than their own. People in so-called 'society' or in politics, diplomacy, finance, business, 'landed gentry' or whatever, would bend over backwards to lionize a celebrity. Many measured their own status by the number and quality of the celebrities they could name as friends."

This turned all of their travels, whether together or singly, into repetitions of their wedding trip. Europe or the Orient—it made no difference—at dockside, railroad station, and hotel entrance the crowds were always huge. And the nights were taken up by receptions given or attended by royalty and princelings. Even in Russia, which they visited in 1926—despite warnings of a possibly hostile greeting—the mobs turned out by day, the ruling elite (in smaller but no less wearying number) by night. One might compare their travels to those of Queen Elizabeth and her consort on a state visit, binding England's ties to her dominions. But of course Doug and Mary's dominion was the whole great world itself.

As a result of all their traveling the Pickfair guest list in the 1920s was a wonder to behold. In the famous gymnasium at his studio the star played leapfrog with Babe Ruth, sparred with Gene Tunney and Jack Dempsey, allowed the King of Siam to ride his mechanical horse, Conan Doyle to punch the bag, the Duke of Alba* to fence with him. Prince William of Sweden, not unnaturally, did Swedish exercises there. Lord Mountbatten spent part of his honeymoon at Pickfair, and at his suggestion Prince George of England, then a serving officer in the royal navy, spent a weekend there when his ship put in at a West Coast port. He had such a good time that he actually went absent without leave for several hours to round out his revels, which included a studio tour where he was encouraged to take a bite out of a window—made out of sugar so that a stuntman could safely crash through it.

Among the other pleasures the prince sampled was a variation

---

* *Some time later, when the "Champagne Cocktail Duke," as the press had dubbed him, was appointed Minister of Education, then, a month later, Foreign Secretary by his hunting companion, the last reigning Spanish monarch, Alfonso XIII, newsmen hustled off to get a reaction from Doug. He did not tell them, as he told friends, than when Alba presented him to Alfonso, the King's first query was about what really happened in the Fatty Arbuckle case. Instead, he issued a lordly statement: "Spain's greatness will be perpetuated as long as it calls to high administrative office such men as Duke de Alba. He is fitted for leadership by personal attainment as well as by his traditions."*

on badminton devised by the star, taught by him to such tennis stars as Tilden, Johnson, and Suzanne Lenglen and called simply, "Doug." * The record does not show whether the future Duke of Kent was treated to a predawn ride through the nearby hills and canyons (subdivision had not yet reached the hills above Los Angeles). But on at least a few occasions, guests at their own request (which some perhaps came to regret) were routed out of bed at an ungodly hour, placed groaning atop horses and taken for a strenuous trot through the darkness to a campsite where breakfast— sent out by truck in advance—would be laid. Steak, Florida grapefruit and *croissants* might be on the menu; the star himself might tell the tale of a legendary bandit, Tiburcio Vasquez, whose hideout, he claimed, had been in the very canyon where they were dining. Or he might have a cowboy quartet on hand to serenade his friends.

Nor, apparently, was the royal figure invited to the camp Fairbanks maintained near Laguna Beach, a couple of hours south of Los Angeles, but not a few distinguished visitors accompanied him to this luxuriously appointed tent site on a quarter-mile stretch of crescent-shaped beach, where they could enjoy the outdoor life without surrendering the comforts of a good bed, excellent cuisine, and the attentions of servants.

Still, it was surely obvious to the prince that there was no end to Fairbanks' interests. Spike Robinson, a boxer who had also served

---

* *The game was played with specially designed heavy shuttlecocks and standard tennis racquets on the usual badminton court and employing that game's high net. It was much faster than ordinary badminton and more furious than ordinary tennis. Howard Hawks, one of several distinguished directors who began their careers under the Pickford-Fairbanks aegis (he worked as an assistant on some of her pre-war films), was often Doug's partner in doubles and recalls that they could generally beat the visiting tennis champions—doubtless because the latter found the rhythms of the new game difficult to master quickly.*

as a sparring partner for Griffith, had now joined Bull Montana on the athletic staff. William A. Wellman, later to be one of Hollywood's leading directors, had first met Fairbanks when he was a scrappy young hockey player in Boston and the actor, working in some road company or other, was impressed by his spirited play. Wellman had flown with the Lafayette Flying Squadron during the war and then looked up Fairbanks when he was barnstorming in California in the Twenties. Fairbanks, of course, was fascinated by flying, went joy-riding with Wellman and, characteristically, encouraged the flyer to look for work in the movies. He also encouraged him to land his plane on the Fairbanks lawn whenever that was convenient. It was among his most delightful traits—the wide-ranging quality of his interests and his quick energy in satisfying them. He was, for example, shocked to discover, when she visited him, that none of Anna Pavlova's dances had been recorded for posterity on film. He immediately arranged a shooting session on the *Bagdad* set. She danced to "remembered" music of her most famous pieces, among them "The Dying Swan" and, indeed, Fairbanks' film remains one of but two visual records of her art. On another occasion, visiting Henry Ford, he encouraged the none-too-spry auto magnate to join him on a climb to the top of Ford's home. Mary and Mrs. Ford emerged from tea to find the men cackling gleefully from the ridgepole. "Perfectly safe," Doug later explained. "I tried the handholds twice before I let him go up."

1. *The Thief of Bagdad* (1924).

2. As Bennie Tucker, "a bellboy" (but also the lead) in Kellett Chalmers' *Frenzied Finance* (1905). An anonymous playgoer wrote in her program: "Douglas Fairbanks simply great."

3. With author-star Tom Wise in another early theatrical success, *The Man from Mississippi*.

4. First film: *The Lamb* (1914).

5. One of the later—and most successful—short comedies, *The Mollycoddle* (1920). The heroine is Seena Owen.

6. An antique caption suggests that this may be the only known photograph of William S. Hart smiling. The young Fairbanks was the man to do it—especially if there was a cameraman present.

7. Best friends: Fairbanks and Charles Chaplin don the gloves (*circa* 1918).

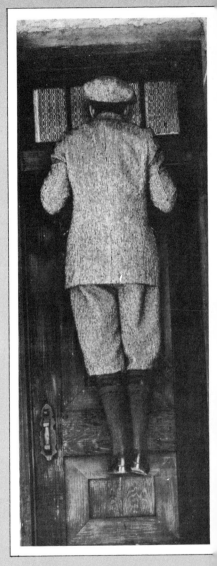

8. The physical culturist working out at the studio (1920).

9. Even when he peeks, Fairbanks stunts. *His Majesty, the American* (1919).

10. Entering history astride proud plug, Fairbanks the indomitable D'Artagnan in *The Three Musketeers* (1921).

11. Swaggering, irrepressible . . . another view of D'Artagnan in *Musketeers.*

12. Borrowing a handy swordsman for a lightning handspring in *Musketeers*.

13. Airborne as *Robin Hood* (1922).

14. Looking and feeling irresistible . . . as
The Thief of Bagdad.

15. The persistent Fairbanks hitching a ride on Julianne Johnston's sedan chair in *The Thief*.

16. A pensive, almost melancholy portrait of *The Thief*.

17. Maxfield Parrish's poster for *Thief*.

18. Mary Pickford, age 10, in a small role in the stage play *The Fatal Wedding* (1903).

19. Pickford—chaste, delicate, child-like—almost a poster girl for the values of her time.

20. As the Madonna in *The Foundling* (1916).

21. In the title role of *Stella Maris* (1918), one of two parts she played in the film.

22. Portrait of Mary.

23. Celebrities in profile: Douglas Fairbanks and Mary Pickford.

24. En route to Europe: Jack Pickford (left), Mary's brother, and Douglas, Jr. say farewell to Mary and Doug.

25. At sea.

26. The veranda at Pickfair, the Fairbanks' nest in Beverly Hills.

27. The enchanted couple considering the plunge.

28. With the Duke of Sutherland, noted sportsman, government official and houseguest *extraordinaire*.

29. The Fairbanks at home.

30. Lawn party: actor Louis Wolheim, author Dr. Karl Vollmoller, Mary as *My Best Girl*, German actor Emil Jannings, Doug as *The Gaucho*, and director (*The Arabian Knights*) Lewis Milestone.

31. A spontaneous little paddle in the pool.

32. *The Black Pirate* (1926).

33. *The Gaucho* (1927).

34. In a merry moment from *The Taming of the Shrew* (1929).

35. With a group of Chinese scholars at Peking (third from right).

36. Father and son.

37. "America's Sweetheart" leaves Los Angeles court-room after having been granted divorce from Doug-las Fairbanks, Sr. (1935).

38. Doug, looking smaller, older, less than merry, returns from abroad to discuss plans for *Marco Polo*, a picture he would not live to make.

39. Doug, with his third wife, Lady Ashley, previously married to Lord Ashley and subsequently married to Clark Gable.

40. Mary with her present husband, bandleader Buddy Rogers (1948).

XII

Yet by the middle of the decade this admirable and cheerful existence was shadowed, and these shadows deepened as the decade wore on—although none but his intimates was permitted to notice them. To the casual observer the fortyish Doug Fairbanks seemed as lithe and quick as ever; only his doctors observed that his circulation was not as good as it might have been and that, perhaps, he was extending himself beyond the limits suitable for a man of his age. Their cautions, it need hardly be said, were scorned by Fairbanks, though the hint of mortality was reinforced around the time he was making *Robin Hood* when his half-brother, John, suffered a stroke. He virtually lost the power of speech; but one day, when Douglas was taking him for a drive, they passed a cemetery and John was able to point to it and say, "Jack there." It threw Douglas into a state of profound depression and he told his brother, Robert, he hoped when death came to him it would strike quickly. "I can't think of anything more horrible than being ill," he said.

There was, however, one thing that seemed just as bad to him—the emergence around this time of his son as a movie player. The Sully family had begun to sell off its jewels and heirlooms to make ends meet. Thus when Jesse Lasky, production chief at Paramount, offered Douglas, Jr., the lead in a film, the opportunity was irresistible. The once-chubby child—his softness was often criticized by his father—had turned into a slender, comely youth. He was beginning to look a great deal like his father. Indeed, in a few years he would surpass him both in looks and in the range of his acting ability, though never in sheer magnetism. So there was reason enough, even without his name, for Lasky to take a flyer on him, although it was the name the producer was buying, he later admitted. Lasky was also buying a chance to irritate Douglas, Sr. And in that he succeeded. Fairbanks made his objections clear to the press—the boy should be in school, he was too young to work, unscrupulous men were trying to use him. In private, he behaved with even less control; he threatened to cut young Douglas out of his will.

Still, the boy really owed nothing to his father, and his mother's family needed the income. Beth and Douglas moved back to Hollywood, and the lad received billing above the title in *Stephen Steps Out*, an adaptation of the Richard Harding Davis story *The Grand Cross of the Crescent*, all about a youth's adventures in the sinister Orient. Although most of the reviewers were kind when the film appeared in 1924, it was a failure, and Douglas was forced to take an extremely modest contract—during the course of which his salary was cut in half. He played small parts in occasional major films, slightly larger ones in B pictures, and had to take on extra work whenever the studio demanded it. He was even hard up enough to earn some money writing titles on the side—once for one of his father's films, without Senior's knowledge. All the while the elder Fairbanks derided his son's talents and criticized his taste in attempting to follow in Dad's footsteps.

Actually, what was bothering him was that his nearly grown-up son reminded him—and, possibly, his public—that Senior was not as young as he once had been. And though they reconciled briefly when they met at the 1924 Olympic games, they stayed on very distant terms throughout the rest of the decade. The older man hated being called "Dad"—"it makes me feel so terribly middle-aged," he complained to Robert Fairbanks. And he upbraided his old friend, actor-director Donald Crisp, for casting Junior in one of his films. "There's only one Fairbanks," he snarled when Crisp defended himself by pointing out that the young man was right for the part and good in it besides.

So he felt assaulted, in middle life, from both ends of the age spectrum and after *The Thief of Bagdad* he faltered as both producer and actor. Its immediate successor was *Don Q, Son of Zorro* and, of course, a sequel to his first great costume success. In comparison to what had gone immediately before it, the film was slightly regressive. The business with the stock whip was good, but it was essentially a stationary skill. And Cooke noted that when he used the whip as a rope to swing to the top of a wall, there was a slight, steadying stumble when he landed. Doubtless he had stumbled before when the cameras were running. But this was the first time he had allowed a less-than-perfect bit of gymnastics to stay in the finished film. Public response was still strong, however, and the reviews were indulgent, if not as fulsome as they had previously been.

His next film, *The Black Pirate*, represented a return to something like his previous scale. There was movement in the ship and the sea and excitement in seeing the Fairbanks energy compressed in the close confines of the pirate vessel. Moreover, it included his most famous and spectacular single stunt—Fairbanks inserting a dagger in the top of a taut sail and clinging to it as it cut rapidly down the canvas. Most important of all, it was the first major experiment with technicolor. At that time Dr. Herbert T. Kalmus' invention was only a two-color process, but Fairbanks and director Albert Parker used it delicately and imaginatively, so that reviewers said the film had the effect of a watercolor, praising the restraint of the producer in not going for bolder, splashier effects. They spoke, as well, of its being yet another example of his "zealous effort toward the esthetic betterment of his profession." The star himself struck a becomingly modest pose when discussing the first true color feature (previous efforts in this direction had depended either on hand coloring each frame of film—these were, perforce, very short films—and on using chemically toned mono- chrome film stock). "Really, I don't know what it's all about, he said, none of us does. That's why it is all so confoundedly interesting."

His next feature, despite a cameo appearance by his wife—as a dream vision of The Madonna—was merely confounded in the eyes of most critics and, when all was said and done, by the star as well. *The Gaucho*, despite Fairbanks' tricks with the bola, was the flattest of his big-scale adventure-romances. Indeed, it is hard to determine just what he thought he was doing here. There was, throughout the 1920s, a considerable popular interest in Latin American themes, settings and characters, so doubtless he thought to take advantage of that interest with this story of Argentinian life. He appears as a sort of Robin Hood figure determined to prevent Ruiz, the Usurper, from robbing a holy shrine of the wealth that has accumulated there (it is a spring, the waters of which have curative powers). He does so, but falls victim of leprosy and is finally healed by the magic waters. Along the way, however, he permitted himself a drunk scene, was shown to be lustful of virgin innocence and, of course, was shown undergoing a spiritual conversion. These made even his best critical friends uneasy. As Robert E. Sherwood wrote: ". . . there is no place for anything but Douglas Fairbanks—and all the beautiful, preposterous qualities that Douglas Fairbanks represents—in a Douglas Fairbanks film." There were, to be sure, some sops for his fans—a splendid cattle stampede, a lovely jailbreak—but on the whole *The Gaucho* was the most disappointing of his features to that time. Eileen Bowser has speculated that he may have been trying to emulate Cecil B. De Mille's commercially successful blends of spectacle and religiosity. One might also see in a film that revolves around religious conversion an attempt to create a variant on his favorite old theme of characterological transformation. One might even see in the movie a crude effort to deal with more "mature" themes than Fairbanks had heretofore essayed. Nevertheless, it seemed to most people to be more tired than inspired, lacking the grace and gaiety, the bounce and drive, associated with his name and work.

In fact, *The Gaucho* was the clearest public evidence yet that Fairbanks had spared not a moment's planning for that most inevitable of contingencies, age. He was completely identified with a screen character who had no capacity built in him to age. This character was rather like Peter Pan; his appeal was based on eternal youth. But he was not, of course, a literary construct, one which could be fleshed out anew by a different player for each succeeding generation. He was Doug and Doug was him. And Doug, alas, was only a man, and a man is condemned to grow old. Moreover, this screen character no longer had any capacity to live in the real world; again, as with Peter Pan, his natural environment was never-never land. Fairbanks could not now reinsert him into the twentieth century, put him back into a business suit, for example, and permit him to play in mature romantic dramas or to be a father figure to younger heroes. *The Gaucho* thus represented his one attempt to show his alter ego aging in character. In his next film he would kill him off and thereafter he would never bring him back to life. All his subsequent films would be experiments with alternatives, none of which proved entirely comfortable to him or attractive either to his old public or to a newer one. There was, one must say, something typically American in his lack of foresight in this matter. Our public life, in every area of endeavor, is full of brave beginnings and feeble endings. We are ever betrayed by the enemy we will not acknowledge—time.

It is perhaps our emphasis on youth not merely as a stage in development but as a value in itself that leads to this betrayal. In the vigor of it we seem to be the initiators, the masters of change. We are ill-prepared to accept changes that time brings—changes in the spirit and interests of contemporaries, changes especially in the physical world around us that are wrought by technological development, shifting values in the political and artistic realms. We want things to be as they were in the days of our glory, which is perhaps why the American popular culture places such a heavy stress on nostalgia.

Fairbanks, besides having to deal at this time with broad hints about his mortality, was also forced to confront changes in his wife and in his art. Mary Pickford was now 34 and though she had just a year before played a young adolescent in one of the best of her features, *Sparrows* (it was about a group of children shamelessly exploited and shamefully treated on a Southern "baby farm" where their parents imagined they were being well cared for), it was now clear to her that it was time to allow her screen character to age somewhat and to permit romance to enter her screen life. Until now all her relationships with the opposite sex on screen had been completely without sexual overtones. Indeed, she had never had a leading man in the conventional sense. Rather, she had mostly appeared as a young girl making her way alone, with occasional assistance from an elderly kinsman or guardian, often encumbered by a younger sibling she was expected to protect. She was not yet ready to play her age, but in *My Best Girl* she would be seen as an older adolescent and one who was falling in love with the boy next door. For this role she chose Buddy Rogers. One day Fairbanks dropped in on her set while they were filming a love scene, glowered at the pair for a while, then spun on his heel and stalked away. "It's more than jealousy," he told his brother Robert, though he was often described as morbidly jealous of Miss Pickford. "I suddenly felt afraid." It was not that Miss Pickford and Rogers were having an affair. It is probably not even that Fairbanks was prescient enough to sense the attraction that would begin to grow between them and culminate in marriage. It was just that he was preternaturally sensitive, as his relationship with his son proved, to all youthful intrusions on what he regarded as his domain. And Rogers, a perpetual juvenile (and sometime band singer), represented yet another threat to him in—how could he deny it?—his middle years. Moreover, he and Miss Pickford had begun almost imperceptibly to drift apart. She shared neither his love for travel nor his love for the out-of-doors. Indeed, it seems she did not like people very much, unless they were part of her small, close-knit group of intimates. "Mary was always the queen up there on the hill," Adela Rogers St. John, the shrewd Hearst journalist who was for a time close to her, later confided to another journalist. She was, according to Mrs. St. John, "the phantom, the legend. I don't know whether it's true Doug Fairbanks wanted to put a wall around Beverly Hills to keep the mortals out. But there was a psychological wall around her and her circle, if not a concrete one." Now, it seemed, she was tired of globe-trotting, tired of the strenuous life, perhaps tiring of Fairbanks' panic over youth's fading. For his part, he felt more and more confined "on the hill," in Hollywood in general. It appears he had some need to assuage his fear of aging by proving that he was still attractive to younger women. Anyway, the marriage was entering on its long phase of terminal tension.

Symbolically—and with an attendant barrage of publicity—Little Mary decided to cut the long golden curls that had been her trademark literally since childhood, giving way to the controversial jazz-age fashion of bobbed hair. It was all for her art, her slightly naughty role in the last of her silent films, *Coquette*, but it was also a signal to "her people" that she would never return to childish roles. And yet another signal to her husband that the times were irreversibly changing.

All of this, unfortunately, coincided with the industrywide anguish over the coming of sound. *The Jazz Singer* went into release at about the same time as *The Gaucho* and, for once, Fairbanks' commercial shrewdness deserted him. Like most of the Hollywood establishment, he hoped that if he did not think about this phenomenon, it would go away. And, in fact, the transitional years of 1927–1928, produced a remarkable final flowering of great American silent films—all of them, in retrospect, finer works of art than any early talkie or part-talkie. Among them were Josef von Sternberg's *The Last Command*, giving Emil Jannings his finest American role; Raoul Walsh's *Sadie Thompson*, in which the director himself starred with Gloria Swanson and Lionel Barrymore; King Vidor's arresting blend of realism and expressionism, *The Crowd*; Victor Seastrom's *The Wind*, in which Lillian Gish had one of the finest of her post-Griffith roles in one of the strangest of all American films; and, finally, Wellman's *Wings*, which received the first Academy Award as best picture of the year.

Fairbanks had been instrumental in organizing the Academy of Motion Picture Arts and Sciences and, appropriately his wife won the best-actress prize for *Coquette* in 1928. The first presentation of little art deco statuettes had taken place in his office at the studio in 1927. It was an unpretentious and even merry occasion—the first and last such in the history of the institution and its awards. It was climaxed by Fairbanks' speculating on whether it was possible to heave one of these new prizes over the high, wide, hangar-like roof of one of the nearby stages. Some of the group repaired thither and, sure enough, the launching turned out to be a success.

But such prankish moments were growing increasingly rare in Fairbanks' life. His career was as threatened by sound as his marriage was by Pickford's increasing withdrawal from participation in the activities that interested him. As for sound, he may have, as his son suggests, "welcomed it for certain types of films," but, like Chaplin, he felt that it was not appropriate for his kind of work. Dialogue, he thought, would break up the smooth arcs of action that were central to the appeal of his films and, to a degree, he was correct, though as the later films of Errol Flynn and his own son showed, there were ways of minimizing this problem. The trouble was that, at the beginning, prevailing wisdom held that the public wanted to hear something—and that something preferably dialogue —coming at them without respite from the sound track. Worse, the early sound equipment required microphones to be hidden about the set and the actors to stay immobilizingly close to them. It also imprisoned the camera in a huge blimp (to prevent the whirring of its motor from intruding on the sound track).

So, given the choice of making his next film, *The Iron Mask*, either as a silent or a talkie, he opted for the former—though there was a spoken prologue and a spoken epilogue and a musical score recorded on the film. His niece-biographer believes that, playing again his beloved D'Artagnan "was his own way of saying farewell to those millions who had shared his adventures and thrilling escapades in a decade of movie-going. It was also an expression of his religious philosophy." At the end, she observes, his old companions in arms, Athos, Porthos, and Aramis—already dead—approach the mortally wounded D'Artagnan. As spirited in death as they were in life, they beckon him to join them. When, finally, he falls, they lift his spirit from the shell of his body and, sensing hesitation, Porthos laughs, "Come on," he says, "there's greater adventure beyond."

There is something brave and touching in Fairbanks, so preoccupied with thoughts of mortality, causing such a scene to be written and performed. Miss Fairbanks quotes Allan Dwan, who directed the film, as saying that the actor was more than usually meticulous in producing this picture. "It was as if he knew it was his swan song," the director commented. Perhaps Fairbanks hoped it would be. Perhaps it should have been. But in fact he had eleven more years to live and circumstances would require of him a less graceful exit from the stage.

Other aspects of his biography indicate that he was preparing for, or at least contemplating, some sort of dignified semiretirement, though he was, in fact, only forty-five and may perhaps have been merely enduring the familiar—and patiently curable—confusions of that as yet unnamed phenomenon, the mid-life crisis.

But patience was never his strong suit. And he was actor enough (and narcissist enough) to enjoy the drama of his situation. At least part of the time. A good bit of the rest of the time in the late Twenties—and on into the Thirties—he devoted to building, on three thousand acres of land in San Diego County, a considerably romanticized and enlarged version of the kind of hacienda that might have stood in such a place when Spain ruled California—had the Spanish Grandees made movie-star money instead of depending on agriculture. By the time Fairbanks took it over, this particular tract had been largely covered with eucalyptus trees from which the previous owner—the Santa Fe railroad—had hoped (fecklessly, as it turned out) to make railroad ties. Fairbanks rechristened the place Rancho Zorro and set about trying to make it into a setting where he could live within his favorite historical fantasy, Spanish California. In the next few years he would turn the grounds into a wonderland, creating artificial pools and waterfalls, turning the forest into a wild-animal preserve. On one early visit to it, Doug and Mary pressed their hands into the soft cement of a new irrigation dam and inscribed their names there, too.

XIII

But time was running out in some senses faster than Fairbanks knew. The depression was just an historical second away and though it would scarcely reduce Fairbanks to poverty, it would strap him sufficiently so that he would have to abandon his plans for a picturesque peasant village to house Rancho Zorro's workers and please its master's eye. Nor would he live long enough to taste the fruits of his new orange groves, nature being almost as slow to mature its products as movie stars are to mature their characters. Still, they existed in his fantasy and when, in England, he one time boasted of the quality of his home-grown oranges and offered to provide his listeners with samples, his brother responded by shipping crates of the fruit bought from another grower whose trees had deeper roots.

So Fairbanks had to content himself with just two fully established establishments in California (he and Mary had a beach house at Santa Monica—called Fairford by their circle—where they could "get away" from the strenuous life of Pickfair). He also found himself, in 1928, participating in a remarkable—and in some sense humiliating—occasion. It was decreed by Joseph Schenck that the major stars releasing through UA should participate in a radio broadcast designed to demonstrate to the public that they had voices good enough to meet the requirements of talking pictures. The cost was $250,000, a fifth of which was divided among the participants as talent fees. The sponsor was Dodge, the car makers. The "studio" was Mary Pickford's bungalow on the lot. Appearing with her and her husband were the other original United Artists, Chaplin and Griffith (now reduced to mere employee status in the company), and Norma Talmadge (Schenck's wife), Dolores Del Rio, Gloria Swanson, and John Barrymore—though why there should have been any doubt about his vocal quality is difficult to imagine. Fairbanks was master of ceremonies and addressed the youth of America in homiletic fashion. Pickford "talked intimately" to women. Miss Del Rio sang "Ramona," Barrymore recited a *Hamlet* soliloquy, Miss Swanson discussed a young girl's chances of "crashing" Hollywood, while Miss Talmadge gave a little lecture on fashion. Griffith discussed "love in all its phases, eschewing the sex angle completely"—which must have made for a rather peculiar speech. Chaplin "nearly died of mike fright."

It is a measure of how serious people regarded the technological revolution in movies that the press—and indeed all UA executives—were barred from the dressing room while the broadcast proceeded, and that wild rumors went around about what had gone on in there—someone had sung for Miss Del Rio, someone had spoken for Miss Talmadge, a not unreasonable supposition since she hated talking in public and followed her sister Constance ("thank God for the trust funds Momma set up") into retirement after just two mediocre talkies. The idols of a decade and more were, it seemed, in trouble. And the Hollywood establishment did little to soothe their understandable anxiety or to reassure their public. Bland press releases didn't do the job; the industry communicated its panic to the world. The trade press ran think-pieces about the end of the star system, predictions that they would all be replaced by "real" (i.e., legitimate) actors, authoritative reports stating that one-third of the movie's players would never work again.

And the dark side of sycophancy and fandom came to the fore. There was a peculiar relish in the way producers declared that certain overpriced temperaments, whose tantrums they had been forced to suffer in silence, whose misbehavior they had devoted hours to hushing up, now turned on many stars with unseemly haste and declared dozens of troublemakers to be "washed up." The public, too, overfed on the notion that the stars were, underneath it all, regular guys and gals, just like the fans, found itself titillated by the possibility that the luck of people who had been made to seem merely lucky was now about to run out.* There was an irresistible rightness, dramatic and psychological, about their situation. Pious

---

* *It is a curious thing, but nearly every successful film or popular novel about movies—*A Star is Born, Sunset Boulevard, The Big Knife, *even that excellent and mostly cheerful musical,* Singin' in the Rain—*revolves dramatically around a falling star. There is some unspoken, unconscious need for a punishing last act in the career drama of the celebrated. It restores our sense of order, our sense that good luck is not lasting, that in the end the rewards of bourgeois virtue and hard work are more permanent. Such dramas, of course, occur quite regularly in show business, but often as not, stars, like other successful people, live out their final years in placid, prosperous retirement.*

tears were shed as people avidly absorbed the news of disasters as absurd as the good fortune that had preceded them. Prestige, wrote the pioneering nineteenth-century sociologist, Gustav Le Bon, is "a sort of domination exercised on our mind by an individual, a work, or an idea." That domination for a while "paralyzes our critical faculty," fills us with "astonishment and respect . . ." But, he observed, it is a force easily blown away. "From the moment prestige is called in question it ceases to be prestige. The gods and men who have kept their prestige for long have never tolerated discussion. For the crowd to admire, it must be kept at a distance." The crowd, alas, was very much in on the discussion of sound and what it was doing to their sometime favorites.

Fairbanks and Pickford decided to combat the threat by combining their prestige, co-starring in *The Taming of the Shrew*, which, of course, attached their names to the greatest dialogue writer in the language. No one could fault the shrewdness of their decision as a career move. The industry's *de facto* leaders seemed to be welcoming the new technology, demonstrating that the addition of sound opened to film vast realms of great drama and literature that heretofore it had never truly been able to encompass effectively. Moreover, Fairbanks was right for the part of Petruchio, while Miss Pickford, struggling still to change her image, was interestingly offcast as the shrew.

The resulting film, however, was not as good as it should have been. Fairbanks' essential egoism was quite suitable for a shrew-tamer, but his voice came through the microphones rather high-pitched, while his wife was less mercurial, perhaps, than she should have been—and had in other roles proved herself capable of being. The production itself, adapted and directed by Sam Taylor, was flat and stagey and carried a now legendary credit, perhaps funnier than anything in the action of the film itself—"By William Shakespeare. Additional Dialogue by Sam Taylor." It was certainly not improved by Fairbanks' behavior on the set. He did not rage at the changes that were being forced on him—that might have been more tolerable. Instead, he sulked. Miss Pickford reports in her autobiography that, though they were both due on the set at 9 A.M., he would stretch his morning exercise and rub-down period until noon, while cast and crew waited, running up charges that deeply offended her frugal, highly professional soul. When he did appear, he often had not memorized his lines and had to have them chalked on a blackboard out of camera range. He also refused to do retakes. It was a very petulant act, and at a moment when everyone was understandably more tense than usual about a production, when— like it or not—careers really were on the line, it had elements of self-destructiveness in it that are still astonishing to contemplate.

His reviews, on the whole, were actually better than his wife's, but the film performed badly at the box office, at least in part because it went into release just as the stock market crashed. That represented another giant step downward on his descent into self-pity, for it challenged all the verities about pluck, luck, and hard work that had formed such intellectual underpinnings as had sustained him. Now, as Mary Pickford was later to put it, "a strange fever and restlessness settled upon him . . ." For the first time he set sail for a foreign adventure without her, taking Tom Geraghty, his screenwriting pal, with him ostensibly to attend the Walker Cup golf matches in Scotland, but really to hide, perhaps cure, the fact that he had never been more psychologically beset. Hurting financially, his films declining in popularity to the nadir represented by *Shrew*, a sense of estrangement (though by no means an open breach) growing between Mary and him, a reconciliation with his son now interrupted because the latter insisted on marrying Joan Crawford against his entire family's wishes (she was not yet the major star she was to be, and was therefore not as socially suitable as she might later have been), this trip established the pattern that would rule the rest of his life—one of aimless globe-trotting punctuated by announcements of grandiose production plans and the release of an occasional feature that neither lived up to those announcements nor to the quality of his past work.

As for Mary, she could not, perhaps would not, be of much help to him. In her autobiography she says that she had always served as Fairbanks' hatchet man (her phrase), taking on the unpleasant duty of informing those who had won his favor—for a project or a part in a picture—that they were the victims of his expansiveness, that they were not to receive whatever boon it was that he had promised them. Now she was tired of that role and exhausted, too, by seeing her mother through a three-year fight against cancer which she had finally lost in 1928. Moreover, she was preoccupied with the struggle to maintain her own career in talking pictures. Douglas, she would later sniff, "always faced a situation the only way he knew how, by running away from it." By contrast, she "always preferred to look an issue squarely in the face."

The one she chose to face while he was away was her third sound film, *Secrets*. When it was finished, it displeased her for reasons that she has never fully disclosed. Perhaps her confidence was, in its way, as shattered as Fairbanks' was, for it was uncharacteristic of Pickford to go this far with a project, then waver and, finally, abandon it, ordering the entire negative burned—a dead loss of $300,000.*

---

* In 1933 she would remake the film, co-starring with Leslie Howard. It went into release during the bank holiday and, though well reviewed, made no money. It was her last film.

Thereafter, she joined Fairbanks abroad, and he shouldered some of the blame for the film's failure . . . if he had not upset her . . . if he had been present to help steady her emotions. He returned and, for the last time, devoted himself seriously to a movie, one that he thought would be more suited to the temper of the times and to his own age than the historical romances—or *Shrew*—had been.

It was a musical, and he did not stint on talent. The score was by Irving Berlin, who also collaborated on the script with director Edmund Goulding—not a top-rank film-maker, but a solid craftsman who came to be known, ironically, as a man with a knack for making pictures capable of arresting a falling star's decline. In the cast were Bebe Daniels, Edward Everett Horton, and a talented young singer named Bing Crosby. But it came out at a moment when the market was beginning to be glutted with musicals, for the success of the first "All Singing, All Talking, All Dancing" films bred an excess of unimaginative imitations of which the public quickly tired. Nor was the film's satire on American tycoonship well received, American tycoonship having just put the nation into a pretty pickle. Finally, an acrobatic sequence seemed forcibly inserted into the story merely so the star could strut his stuff—and tired, strained stuff at that.

Fairbanks was not unaware of the film's defects. Indeed around that time he gave an interview to a visiting journalist complaining about the way movies had slowed down since the microphones had appeared on the set. He told the man—quite correctly—that only the Mickey Mouse cartoons had so far demonstrated the artistic potential of the sound film. "These cartoons get their tremendous appeal from the perfect rhythm, in comedy tempo, of the little characters and of the accompanying sound. It is not merely synchronization; it is more than that; it is a rhythmic, swinging, lilting thing, with what musicians call the proper accent-structure." He had heard that Sergei Eisenstein, the Russian master, was trying to adapt his famous theories of montage to the sound film and he hoped that they would be able to meet in Paris that year, since he felt Eisenstein was "the only man who seems to be thinking along the same lines as myself." He explained: "Eisenstein contends that the only vital force that can be translated through a combination of sound and movement is rhythm. Therefore he uses varying rhythms to get his effects; drama, comedy, tragedy all have a different rhythm."

His interlocutor thought his enthusiasm "more impressive than his logic," though now, with Eisenstein's theories safely academicized, it is apparent that the actor understood them well enough, even though what he was repeating was a version of them transmitted from H. G. Wells to Ivor Montague to Fairbanks. It is also obvious, from other remarks he made at the time, that he saw more clearly than the rest of Hollywood that the best response to the challenge of the soundtrack was not merely to photograph stage plays or to make one musical after another. "Just as Griffith showed us the essence of the silent picture technique in *Birth of a Nation*, someone is going to create a standard of talking-picture method," he said, strongly implying that he wanted to be that man.

Here, however, was the essence of an important aspect of the celebrity problem. His position gave him ready access to the upper levels of the artistic and intellectual world (Eisenstein to Wells to Fairbanks), and he was intelligent enough, vital enough, to want to test the practical value of the abstract ideas he picked up as he made his way through that bright world. He was not, however, the intimate of these celebrity peers—not really. They did not so much collect one another as rent one another for brief periods of mutual display. In the end, the intellectuals and artists, doubtless refreshed and stimulated by their contact with the people of the more public professions, retired to their studies and studios, to that privacy denied performers of Fairbanks' unprecedented rank.

He, however, had no one to turn to. The business leaders of his industry were as troubled and as insecure as he was. They were coping with the problems of a new technology and greatly changed economic conditions, too. And with no better sense of direction than Fairbanks. As for his intimates, his entourage, they were no help at all. They could not say nay to his escapist whims. And about the significant issues that must have nagged at him daily, in the midst of the pleasurable rounds he never ceased, they could offer no sober suggestions or coherent plans. They were employed to help him cope with the small problems of life—getting through the day—not with large ones like straightening out careers and marriages and major psychological crises.

It should be remembered that he was a born public personality; that, like almost every actor, he had no real choice as to profession. But the person who must live in public or not really live at all is, almost by definition, a person with little capacity for objective, analytical thought, no taste for the one condition necessary for that mode—solitude. Actors, of course, are self-absorbed; of necessity they study themselves all the time, study the effects they are making. If they pay serious attention to anyone else it is another form of study—for mannerisms they can imitate, or use in the creation of a character. But even that information does not become real until they take it over and figure out some way to give it back to us as their own. Even if they like to be alone, theirs is a communal profession, one which is bound to train that capacity out of them. Moreover, movie stars—excepting such rare ones as Paul Muni or perhaps Marlon Brando—cannot lose themselves in a part; their careers depend on working within an extremely narrow range, the range which is familiar to their public. Nor can they lose themselves in a performance on occasion as a stage actor, toying with his characterization to stave off the boredom of a long run, responds to some variation thrown at him by a fellow player or to the stimulation of an especially attentive audience. Even a long movie is a short run by the standards of the profession—and one that proceeds with no audience to speak of. Then, too, the work is done in short takes, giving the actor little opportunity to warm up, lose himself in his work, and thus find something new in the part and therefore in himself. And there is a final irony about all this. As a rule the screen actor puts in a full work day on the set in order to create perhaps two or three minutes of usable footage. Mostly they stand around and sit around, waiting for technicians to do their work, trying to keep their energy up for those few key moments, fighting ennui at all times. Furthermore, it is generally a long time between pictures (as we have seen, Fairbanks made only one film a year after 1919). Thus, people whose natures cry out for gregariousness, for play, for the center of attention, are left with endless empty hours, days, weeks, months to fill, yet have less natural capacity to occupy that time profitably than anyone else. That is one of the reasons why deals and dealing fills so much time in the movie business—it is something to do, something to talk about, something to kill the empty hours. That is part of the reason why Fairbanks preoccupied himself with Rancho Zorro, why his successors have purchased remote islands in Tahiti (getting there alone can take weeks) or have demonstrated obsessive interest in ranches and resorts and god-knows-what other complicated development projects. The money is there, of course, needing tax shelters in recent decades, but the main thing is that they create so much busy work. The need for it also accounts for much show-biz political activity, for those extensive entourages, for Byzantine social and sexual dealings—a divorce between a couple of major stars can require as much negotiating manpower as a peace treaty between two medium-sized warring powers. Everybody in the star's train may have a real job, but transporting the bunch from home to location to resort to business venture—or just keeping in touch with them if you're going solo—fills many a merry hour. And, of course, when the crowd is around they provide that thing which an actor always needs—an audience.

All of which is a way of noting that actors—stars—though the center of the modern celebrity system, are also its perfect victims. All the other artists must get away from it—to write, to compose, to work out at the *barre* or work on their fingering or whatever. The same is true of the athletes who must always go back to their strangely impenetrable world for their long seasons. Similarly the politicians and business leaders cannot long absent themselves from their shops. Only the actors are as idle as the idle rich who serve as the dress extras of the celebrity world, only they have the time to jet off to Switzerland for the skiing or to charter a yacht to cruise the Greek isles or simply to laze about St. Tropez. The temptations are omnipresent, and succumbing to them is only human.

In the summer of 1930, with gossip about a separation from Mary and retirement from movies circulating, Fairbanks vehemently denied both. "You mustn't listen to talk in Hollywood," he said. "The idlers have nothing to do but spread rumors, and busy people can't spend all their time denying them." Actually, he added, "I was never as interested in pictures as now." He was just contemplating new directions, that's all.

And doubtless he was—part of the time. But the pull of self-pity was powerful—there was a role to be found in that emotion which he had never played. "Aw, Mary," Fairbanks said, "nobody cares anything about us any more, let's sell Pickfair and move to Switzerland and just get old," he said. On another occasion he told her, "When a man finds himself sliding down hill he should do everything to reach bottom in a hurry and pass out of the picture."

She replied that you didn't have to slide if you were willing to climb, but the only climbing left in him was of the social variety and even that seemed more than usually graceless in a middle-aged man, living in the midst of a worldwide depression.

XIV

One August night in 1930, Doug and Mary were staying at the beach house. Just before retiring, Doug came downstairs to leave a note for the servants. There he found himself confronting a young man, a handkerchief covering the lower part of his face, a revolver in one hand, quietly ransacking the house. "Oh, gee, it's Doug Fairbanks," the youthful crook exclaimed, then explained, "I hate to do this, but I must have money."

Ah, the advantages of fame. Fairbanks didn't quite press his autograph on the lad, but he was able to reason sweetly with him, get him to take a companion who was standing watch outside, at a cost of a handful of fives and tens he happened to have in his pocket, thus protecting several thousand dollars' worth of jewelry Mary had in the house. The man departed, apologizing for his intrusion, and Fairbanks didn't even bother to inform the police. Word of the incident merely got around among movie people and finally reached the press, who obtained confirmation from the star by reaching him the following afternoon at the Riviera Country Club, where he was indulging his new—and somehow inappropriately stodgy—passion for golf with "Jayar," as he had taken to calling Douglas, Jr. (He had solved the problem of Dad's dislike for the term "Dad" by calling him "Pete.")

The incident with the admiring thief may not have been the first time Douglas Fairbanks was called upon to protect hearth and home, but it certainly was the last, for the history of his final decade on earth is one long travel itinerary. He didn't wait around to see the reviews of *Reaching for the Moon*. In December he set sail for the Orient, first leg on a round-the-world voyage that would last over six months. Accompanying him were a new athlete-companion Chuck Lewis, a football and decathlon star, and Victor Fleming, the cameraman-turned-director (he would later be known as the man who could "handle" notoriously insecure Clark Gable and director of *The Wizard of Oz* and *Gone with the Wind*). En route, Fairbanks set a world record for the longest ship-to-shore telephone conversation—7,400 miles from his ship four days out of Honolulu to his wife's suite at the Sherry-Netherlands in New York. A couple of weeks later he received a triumphant welcome in Tokyo—did he travel so much because foreign crowds greeted him with an enthusiasm not to be found any more at home?—and a journalist commented that "It is striking to see how all of young Japan,

aristocrats as well as hoi polloi, worship at the Fairbanks shrine."
He attended ju-jitsu and swordplay exhibitions and commented that
the faces he encountered were "vivid with feeling" instead of "blank
and inscrutable" as they had seemed on former visits. Then it was
on to India for the shooting—three leopards, a tiger, and a panther
shot from elephant back. By late spring he had worked his way to
England, where he and Mary had planned to meet. She found "an
elaborately fitted motor car" awaiting her on the dock at
Southampton, a gift from her wayward spouse, and she took it for a
trial spin to Reading, where she met the train bearing him in from
the west country. They stayed on together for two weeks of the
debutante season, then traveled on to Holland and Norway before
returning home, where Fairbanks announced that he "would not
make any more motion pictures based on fiction, plays, or novels."

He had, he would have the world know, solved the problem
of talking pictures, though his solution was scarcely Eisensteinian.
"I am now completing a travel picture of my experiences in my
recent tour of the world, and I believe it will be far superior in
entertainment than any fictional romance I could make. As to the
future, I plan to appear only in films recording my travels." Here,
indeed, was a form of ego-tripping—the camera contemplating the
star contemplating, among other things, the Taj Mahal by
moonlight.

Still, *Around the World in Eighty Minutes* had a certain minor,
forgettable charm. Fairbanks used a golf club as a pointer when
lecturing at a map and by a skillful use of trick photography he
seemed to stride from continent to continent. There were also jokes
about his golf mania, his attempts to manipulate chopsticks and
generally to ingratiate himself with foreign cultures. There was
even a modest thrill or two in the hunting sequences. There was a

general feeling that the narration, written by his friendliest critic, Robert E. Sherwood, set a suitable and novel tone. When it was released in the fall of 1931 *Time* might note that it was "Pictorially . . . nothing much," but felt compelled to add that "the cinema has always before treated information as a bore; travelogues have almost without exception been sad and spiritless"; this one, by contrast, was "witty and de luxe, the record of a trip which must have been fun and of a personality which is happy, egoistic, alert."

In short, the little picture had fulfilled its purpose. It had occupied a year pleasantly, had given point to what might otherwise have been an aimless jaunt—Fairbanks apparently decided to attempt to turn Fleming's home movies into a theatrical feature while *en route*—and it had provided an inexpensive and relatively painless way of meeting his United Artists partners' demands that he continue to contribute to its release schedule whether he liked sound movies or not. Some critics and some members of his public regarded the film as a rip-off of sorts, but most continued to indulge Doug. At forty-eight, he was still—to the older generations of movie-goers, anyway—that perpetually engaging figure, the show-off adolescent, while to younger fans he was merely irrelevant, one of those odd figures their parents were always talking about and harbored some inexplicable affection for. Costing little, the picture made a little. And seemed to reassure Fairbanks briefly that some sort of future might be available to him.

Anyway, the fall found him ebullient and full of plans. In November he and Mary came east where he joked with reporters about his stocks having "fallen arches" ("I told you to stay out of the market," one of them heard Mary say), told them that he wanted to do another travelogue—this time about South America—while Mary might do a play, trying it out in Los Angeles before bringing it in to New York. If, that is, she could find a suitable vehicle. He seemed, said one of the newsmen, "as always, a young man in haste."

He and Mary appeared at the White House to present the first two tickets for Motion Picture Week, during which theaters throughout the country would give special benefit performances, the proceeds going to local relief organizations. Having done his bit for charity, he then bought all ten seats on the airliner back to New York so that his party of five would not have to share space with strangers. A few weeks later he was on the high seas again. His destination, however, was not South America, but the South Pacific (and ultimately Europe), his traveling companions this time including Lewis Milestone, the director, and Robert Benchley, the writer, who was beginning his transition from the New York headquarters of show biz literati—the Algonquin Round Table—to the west coast branch—at the Garden of Allah, once Nazimova's mansion, now a raffish-by-reputation hostelry catering to writers serving well-paid time in the studios. What emerged from this preliminary voyage was a notion to make a new version of a familiar story, eventually entitled *Mr. Robinson Crusoe* and eventually written by Geraghty and directed by a cheerful Hollywood character named Eddie Sutherland, who was responsible for a lot of pleasantly remembered lightweight entertainments.

Though Fairbanks later told reporters that he had loved the Crusoe story since he was a boy and had cherished the notion of doing something with it on the screen for years, one cannot help but think that a more significant reason for the choice of story—the Fairbanks character goes to the island to win a bet that a man can survive alone, without tools or weapons—and location—Tahiti—was that he could use it to prove to his brother, who was complaining about its drain on his finances, that his huge yacht should be regarded as a necessity, not a luxury. Anyway, Fairbanks and his crew lived aboard it (no professional actors were required for the South Sea sequences), had a genuine adventure when it was nearly wrecked on a reef during a storm, and came back with a picture probably cheaper than the travelogue had been, and quite free of the dialogue he hated. They also brought back a young woman named Maria Alba, whom Fairbanks had "discovered" in the islands and who played "Saturday," his native friend. Miss Pickford delivered herself of no comments about her husband's co-star and yachting companion, but Fairbanks was full of praise for the simple life of the South Seas. You could live there for nothing—or for 90 cents a week if you insisted on tobacco and rum. Extras were available for a dollar a day, supplied their own grass skirts and though they had heard of Hollywood and were eager to work there, "somehow one has the yearning to tell them—'Stay where you are.' "

The picture was released in September and the *Times* thought it done "in Mr. Fairbanks' best vein . . . artful, jolly, and imaginative," though most critics and the public paid it scant heed. He, however, had decamped again—this time for Japan, where he played in its national open golf championship, and Tibet, where authorities prohibited him and naturalist Roy Chapman Andrews from hunting for the long-haired tiger and the panda. Instead he settled for a safari through Indo-China and the long way home—through the Suez Canal to Europe, then England, then New York. He was at Pickfair for Christmas. Mary gave him a mahogany bar that had been sent around Cape Horn for use in the Union Saloon in Auburn, California. She had, according to the press, employed two pioneers from the gold-rush days to locate the object.

There was something pathetic in the gesture, since Fairbanks had for three years been pressing his notion of selling Pickfair and not even this handsome gift, associated with the history he found most romantic, was likely to dissuade him. It was not just that the life of the great house now bored him, not just that he would rather spend his money in more mobile pursuits, not even that by this time he was frequently seen in the company of "a woman of nobility" (as the discreet press called her) when he was in Europe. Mostly it was that "Hipper," as he often called his wife and, even since her mother died, had taken to acting more and more the *grande dame.* Although her last picture, the final version of *Secrets,* was about to be issued, the fact was that if his way of coming to terms with the end of their reign at the top was to run and keep running, hers was to withdraw into dignified semi-seclusion. Mrs. St. John recalls a Sunday afternoon when Joan Crawford and Douglas, Jr., were visiting the beach house and they mentioned a dance contest going on at a nearby pier. Douglas, Sr., was all for dropping in on it. Mary wouldn't hear of it. Such things were simply not done.

There was irony upon irony in this. She who had never had a childhood as most people know it—having gone to work as an actress literally before she could read the parts she played—and sustained the image of a child until she was in her mid-thirties, now, strangely, was rushing headlong into matronhood. Her life was like one of those unfortunate films or novels in which we feel the author's time sense is off kilter, but can't quite precisely identify where or why he has gone wrong.

It was increasingly apparent that she could not live easily with her past history. It disturbed her that she could no longer receive the sacraments of her church. It disturbed her, apparently, that she had given so much of herself to her career, including any sense of fun about herself and her life. It may even have been—Catholic puritan that she was—that she felt the long torment of her mother's last illness was a chastisement for them both, for the singlemindedness with which they had pursued security at the expense of everything else. Now she was confronted with the end of the career that had filled her life and with the end of the marriage for which she had sacrificed her religion. Finally, early in 1933, her younger brother, Jack, whose first wife had died a suicide, whose second marriage (to Marilyn Miller) had ended in divorce, whose career as an actor may well have been blighted by her own overwhelming success and who had become an alcoholic, died suddenly, far from home in Paris, in a hotel room from which he could see the hospital in which his first wife had died.

It was all too much. And her response was one about which we can only speculate. Intimates have suggested that Miss Pickford was herself not entirely immune to the bottle at this time (that, indeed, all the Pickfords including the redoubtable matriarch resorted to it frequently) and that Mary's reclusiveness had to do with drinking. It may even be that this was a factor in sending Douglas away on his wanderings. Be that as it may, it does seem that, if she could have managed it, she would have wiped out all memory of her previous public life, reconstituted herself on the spot as simply another wealthy, middle-aging doer of good charitable works, rarely referring to the source of her wealth in "entertainment," trying—or seeming to try—to accomplish in a single lifetime what the possessors of other great fortunes required several generations to do—wipe out the taint attached to the less than socially impeccable means by which they were initially acquired. In years to come she would have to be dissuaded by friends from destroying those of her movies which she controlled. She would publish an inspirational book, *Why Not Try God?* that, like her autobiography, would have strong spiritualist overtones—departed spirits seeming to be with her in the room during moments of crisis and sentiment or appearing to her in dreams to talk things over.

In the weeks of her deepest grief over her brother's loss, however, her husband took off again, this time for St. Moritz, the Riviera, and a visit to Italy. There was talk of proceeding to China to make another movie, but Mary finally joined him in Italy, where, it would seem they talked openly for the first time of his sexual indiscretions. At any rate, she abruptly broke off her stay and preceded him back to Los Angeles. When he returned he found her absent. Buddy Rogers was opening an engagement at the World's Fair in Chicago and she had gone there to visit him. Dosed with his own medicine, Fairbanks responded with an emotional start. He decided to fly to Albuquerque and join her train there, hoping to effect a reconciliation. Driving to the airport, his brother handed him a birthday present—it was, coincidentally, Fairbanks' fiftieth—from his nephews. He opened the box and a mechanical butterfly flitted out and fluttered around the car. In his chastened mood, Doug saw the symbolic appropriateness of the gift. Fairbanks and Pickford reconciled briefly. Then in June, 1933, Fairbanks decided he wanted to return to England again, ostensibly for another golf tournament. His wife saw him off on the boat in New York, but a couple of weeks later received a cablegram from him in which he announced his intention of staying permanently in England and telling her that if she wished to keep Pickfair she might, but that henceforth he would not be responsible for any bills connected with running the place.

There was, obviously, an element of maneuver in all this, for they still cared greatly about each other and were entirely aware of what their marriage symbolized to millions of people, and how messy and undignified a separation would be. His threat to withdraw from responsibility for Pickfair was obviously a ploy to pry her out of the place. Her flight to Rogers' side—his youth, his damnable youth, was in itself an affront to Fairbanks—was doubtless a deliberate assault on his previously unassailed pride in possession of America's Sweetheart.

It may be that her next move, public acknowledgment that rumors of their marital difficulties had substance, was also a calculated maneuver. In her autobiography she claimed that she thought she was talking privately to an old friend when she showed Louella Parsons Doug's cable and announced flatly that she and Doug were parting. Miss Parsons' memory was otherwise. She claimed that though she was "too shocked to think—much less to speak," she acceded to "brave little Mary's" request that she break the news. "The sooner it is known the better. Louella, you are an old friend. You may write the story." It is, indeed, absurd to believe that Mary Pickford, wise in the ways of publicity, didn't know the inevitable results of confiding information to Lolly Parsons, old friend or not. Quite clearly, she was sending a message to Douglas across the waters.

The story rated a two-column headline at the top of the *New York Times* front page the next day, and to the end of her career Miss Parsons rated it as her biggest scoop, bigger even than her breaking the story of their impending marriage fourteen years before. Fairbanks, however, was not available for immediate comment. He was weekending with the Prince of Wales.

Nor was anything else directly forthcoming from him. For the first time in his life he was seen scuttling down fire escapes to evade reporters, and when he finally spoke it was to announce plans to form, with his son and with Alexander Korda, a major production company in England. He told the press that he had seen a preview of Korda's *Private Life of Henri VIII*, thought it was one of the finest films ever made, and felt Korda was the man to supervise his return to the production of important and expensive films. There was talk of taking a long-term lease on a studio, even talk of Fairbanks becoming a British subject. Within a month there was an announcement that Sr. and Jr. would co-star in something called perhaps *Zorro Rides Again* or *Zorro and Son*.

The British were ecstatic. "We Take Film Lead," said one headline. "England Takes World Lead in Pictures," said another. Even the usually sober Manchester *Guardian* editorialized on "The Decline of Hollywood." Back in the United States, where journalists had learned to somewhat discount Fairbanks' grand, optimistic, and endless announcements of future plans, reaction was more restrained. The *Times* commented mildly that the jubilation seemed "somewhat premature . . . merely on the strength of Mr. Fairbanks' first announcement." Such, however, was the power of even a fading world-class celebrity on a society that had no theater folk of comparable fame—though, of course, it had many of comparable, indeed far greater, talent.

In fact, little more was heard of this venture. Fairbanks did succeed in getting Korda's films released in the U.S. through United Artists, and Douglas, Jr. did make several films in England in the late Thirties and again in the early Fifties. It was a pleasant haven for him at a couple of troubled points in his career. Finally, as we shall see, Douglas, Sr., would make his last film there, with Korda producing.

But in the end no mighty new production company rose up in

England to challenge the American giants, which continued to dominate the screens of the world until after 1945 (and for all the more persuasive recent talk of Hollywood's decline, still do). Instead, Mary filed a suit for divorce in Los Angeles the following December. There would be no contest. Each owned their stocks, bonds, and real estate separately. The only property they shared was Pickfair and the physical plant of the United Artists Studio. Fairbanks gladly deeded his share of the former item over to Mary, and shrewd Joe Schenck quietly handled an amicable settlement of the second. The grounds for the divorce were to be "incompatibility" and, it seemed, the word was never more accurately employed.

Or was it? In February 1934, Douglas Fairbanks was named co-respondent in a divorce suit filed in London by Lord Ashley, thirty-four-year-old heir to the Ninth Duke of Shaftesbury. Named with him, at last, was the mysterious "woman of nobility" of the tabloids—Lady Ashley, the former Sylvia Hawkes—tall, blonde, thirtyish, and a one-time chorus girl or "musical comedy star," depending on how friendly the account of the proceedings of the next few months. Mary Pickford now had the means to avenge herself spectacularly. Fairbanks called from London, reaching her in Boston, where she was completing a personal appearance tour, to inquire anxiously into her response to Ashley's charges. She reassured him. She would not escalate the scandal—at least in public. He was properly grateful. And, outraged at Lord Ashley's ungentlemanly behavior, dragging his wife's name through the courts and the public prints in this manner. "He is mad through and through about this thing," Douglas, Jr., told inquiring reporters, while his father's solicitors warned him not to risk contempt of court by commenting publicly on Lord Ashley's charges.

The noble gentleman was, one must say, the perfect figure of a cuckold—soft and dull-looking under his bowler hat. He was also the exemplar of an antediluvian mode of thought, in which one sought "satisfaction" when honor was outraged, in which the power to inflict scandal on the errant was an ultimate weapon, employed only as a last resort, but when employed supposed to break the victims under the weight of their shame and thus preserve—through their tragedy—the proper order of things. How could a member of the squirearchy be expected to understand a world which had set aside such concepts, where the truly gentlemanly thing to do was to arrange quietly such matters as separation and divorce? Fairbanks, the democrat-as-gentleman, understood how these things were supposed to work. Why, thirteen years ago—when it was ever so much more difficult—when no one had heard of Huxley and Waugh and Fitzgerald and all the other novelists who had both demonstrated and satirized the ways things now went in the right circles, he and Mary had managed a similarly sticky situation perfectly. No wonder he was outraged.

Worse, Lord Ashley's action backed him into a corner. For he confessed to intimates that he still had hopes of winning Mary back and she, it appears, was not entirely unwilling to work something out. The trouble was, as Douglas, Jr. was later to say, relations between them "had become a tragic competition [as to] whose pride had been most hurt and who would give in first." A long silence now ensued as Fairbanks worked on what would turn out to be his last film, the working title of which was, ironically, *The Exit of Don Juan*.

The word from America was not good. "The rift with Mary Pickford has cost him a large amount of popularity on this side of the water," a Hollywood "scribe" pontificated, "while it has revived

Mary's popularity, amply demonstrated by the box office returns on her personal appearance tour . . ." That rather oversimplified matters. And failed to credit him with what even Mary would later admit—that he had never ceased to love her, that his need to roam was motivated by feelings both larger and more amorphous than could be contained in a word like "rift." He was, it is fair to say, in revolt against a style of life that he had, to be sure, conspired in creating, but the full ramifications of which were, of necessity, unclear not only to him but to everyone else involved in it. These included very nearly the whole society, down to the dullest wit mumbling moralistically about life in Hollywood while avidly pursuing each scrap dropped from the groaning board of gossip. All the voyagings, all the romantic complications had been attempts to assert his right to freedom, his right to privacy, his right to be himself in the way other wealthy and successful men were permitted to be. Had he been content to live out his life quietly, pottering about Pickfair like some aging democratic monarch, he would have been all right. Had he enjoyed a mental discipline to match his physical discipline, he might even have aspired to some kind of elder-statesman status. That, alas, was not his nature.

And, now, loving Sylvia not less, but Little Mary more, he risked one last rebuff, risked looking like the aging adolescent he was, by returning to Hollywood to sue Mary for the favor of reconciliation. He talked to the New York press when he landed—but not about private matters. Instead he regaled them with stories of his adventures a year earlier in China, to which he had returned to look into making a movie—naturally an "epic"—about Marco Polo. He talked of meeting a warlord who held the opium trade "in the hollow of his hand." He told of smoking the dreaded drug without suffering any ill effects. He talked of Morocco and Marrakesh, of Fez and Rhabat, exotic places visited on the voyage out and the voyage back. And he appeared "in the best health and spirits."

XV

In Hollywood, however, he refused to see the press, always a sensible plan considering the quality of the journalism practiced there. And it responded characteristically by questioning his motives. "Hollywood sentiment has it that he has come to patch things up with Mary, realizing that she alone can rehabilitate him with his more than a little estranged public . . . He has a new picture . . . and would like it to be a success . . ." Such cynicism! He was, in fact, only "mildly interested" in *Don Juan*, had done it mostly as an excuse to stay in England the previous year, while "enjoying his quasibachelorhood and a new kind of 'high life' he had never before experienced," according to his son. He really wasn't much interested in acting any more and in discussing *Marco Polo* made it clear that he would not star in it. If he was to remain active in movies, it would be as a producer, and since *Don Juan* would only marginally affect his prosperity and since, of all his films, it bore the lightest stamp of his creativity, its performance at the box office could not affect his plans.

No, he really hoped to win his wife back. And the day he arrived they met and drove to the beach house. On the way "they were recognized by several other members of the film colony, who reported them apparently happy and joking." Outward appearances were deceiving, according to Mary's reminiscences. She thought "something was gone. It was as though his spirit had fled." Still, they dined together that night at Pickfair. The next day they took lunch and dinner together, with a drive in between, and there must have been some spark between them still. For at the end of the first day together she had merely confirmed their meeting, adding, "Whether I shall see him again is in the lap of the gods." Now she expanded a bit. "I am so very glad that Doug is back. His work always means so much to him. I am sure he will be happy here—now. The future must work itself out and it will. I just cannot bring myself to talk about these things that lie so near to my heart." Whereupon Fairbanks took off for Rancho Zorro alone, but thought better about it and went back for Mary.

The situation appeared to be salvageable, but Mary could not bring herself to entirely accept his protestations of future fealty. Worse, to the public he seemed little more than a faintly absurd roué and the newspaper photographs of him, heavy and balding, and very often glaring angrily at the camera, confirmed their direst suspicions. The contrast with his previous image—lithe and clean-spirited, perpetually youthful, cheery, decently romantic—was unbearable. They did not turn against him, but they did turn away from him. They felt betrayed. And, not unreasonably, his wife shared that feeling. He would have to prove himself with more than words.

So he departed again. Some of the reviews of *The Private Life of Don Juan*—as his last picture was finally called—were quite good. It was a satirical account of what might be termed the Don's sunset years, in which the women he encounters find the reality of him a disappointment compared to the image he had presented in his famous autobiography. Lavishly produced, it was called by *Time* a "wry and glittering comedy of bed-manners which civilized audiences should enjoy." But the ad campaign was deceptive—it led people to think the film represented a return to his previous adventure-romance mode. Worse, it uncomfortably reminded them of the new, new Fairbanks they had been reading about, and that was a form of realism they did not want or need. They stayed away from it.

And Fairbanks stayed away from the United States. In the fall Lord Ashley won his divorce. A little later Mary finally took out her first papers in Los Angeles. By February Fairbanks was organizing a round-the-world cruise with Lady Ashley. Newsmen caught up with them at a London railroad station where they were boarding a train for a channel port, and he put on a sorry exhibition "dodging behind pillars and stands in an effort to keep far away from his titled friend to prevent their being photographed together." He was, the papers said, "in a frightening mood. Three times he threatened violence, twice offering to punch the nose of anyone approaching and once proposing a swing for the jaw."

They got as far as Batavia, in Indonesia, when Fairbanks jumped ship, ostensibly because of a crisis at United Artists, where Joe Schenck was resigning, taking his Twentieth Century unit, responsible for most of the company's releases, out and into a merger with Fox. Again there were talks with Mary; again they were inconclusive. What was required, according to his niece-biographer, was "only the right word, the earnest action, some well-remembered gesture to sweep away the barriers of pride and stubbornness—and for this they both waited."

"World-weary, dissipated" are her words for Fairbanks at this time, though actually it seemed that he had lost touch with reality as it is commonly understood. He was now completely lost in the celebrity dream, unable to find his way back to the kind of words, actions, gestures his niece spoke of. Still all-powerful in his own narrow circle, which he now transported everywhere with him, he seems simply to have refused to believe that he was not omnipotent, that his will was no longer all-powerful. He left Hollywood for England in a few weeks, thinking apparently that Mary would never allow their divorce to become final.

But she did—in January of 1936—although he refused to accept that, either, and he arrived in New York, intending to go on to Hollywood and make one last plea to Mary. He spent a few days there, mostly in the company of Douglas, Jr., sending long wires to Mary. They went unanswered. Impulsively, despairingly, he booked passage for Europe without telling his son, merely leaving a message to forward any important communications via ship-to-shore telegram. Douglas, Jr. went around to the Waldorf, where his father had been staying, and there discovered a wire from Mary indicating a willingness at last to discuss a reconciliation. A clerk had mislaid it. Doug, Jr. excitedly called his father, who refused to believe him. "He felt that his friends and I were merely trying to trap him . . . make him 'jump through hoops,' as he was fond of saying he was obliged to do." Even Mary placed a call to him on the ship, but for once he stayed with his original plan. He refused to return. "It's too late. It's just too late," he told her. On March 7, 1936, he finally married Sylvia in Paris.

Less than a year later, he and Mary were at a United Artists meeting and he prevented her from leaving for a moment. "Don't go out now, Hipper; you'll run into our current wife." At a party where they all found themselves, the two women finally did meet. Mary, with self-conscious graciousness, asked to be presented to

Sylvia. The latter responded by bringing her tea and sandwiches. They exchanged small talk, Sylvia expressing sorrow to hear that Pickfair was on the market. "Pickfair has served its purpose," replied Mary. "Somehow material things do not mean as much to me as they once did." Touché—though of course she still resides on the top of the hill.

Fairbanks by this time had gone into partnership with Samuel Goldwyn to produce his Marco Polo picture. "I have never been an actor, really," he told a visiting journalist. "I've just been kidding the public all these years. I'm a businessman; always have been. Producing is my line."

Well, not really. Fairbanks had wanted his son to star in the film but it could not be worked out and the part went to Gary Cooper. A little later Fairbanks sold out all interest in a project he had been nursing most of the decade. There was talk of yet another new company in which he would produce his son's pictures; a couple of titles were even bandied about in the papers. But nothing came of them. Still, if there existed some happiness for Fairbanks during this last decade of his life, it was certainly in the steady warming in his relationship with his son; his attempts to produce pictures for him reflect a desire, at last, to fulfill some of his fatherly obligations. The disapproved marriage to Joan Crawford had broken up in 1933. More important, Douglas, Jr. had proved himself to be a capable actor and a popular personality in his own right. He had given a splendid performance as Garbo's dissolute younger brother in *A Woman of Affairs*, a version of Michael Arlen's enormously successful romance of the 1920s—it was his last silent film, and hers. He had followed that with strong supporting performances in such early sound movies as Howard Hawks' *Dawn Patrol* and Mervyn LeRoy's *Little Caesar*, where he was thoroughly convincing when cast against type as a gigolo. He had also been an effective straight leading man opposite Katharine Hepburn in *Morning Glory* (for which she won her first Academy Award). If he was not the man his father had been, he was instead his own man, an actor of range and style. (If anything, he was perhaps too much under the influence of his friends, John Barrymore and later Ronald Colman— that is to say, a trifle too carefully well-spoken. He was clearly not beholden to his father for his substantial success. And even better, the two shared other interests. The younger man could always be enlisted in some companionable game; like his father, he was completely at home in the upper levels of international society and he possessed the same desire to move about the world, a lack of rootedness that, of course, suited the older man's mood.

In the mid-thirties Douglas, Jr.'s career suffered a brief decline. When Warner Brothers, in one of its periodic spells of cost-consciousness, refused to renew his rather expensive contract, he decided to free-lance, rather than sign on elsewhere, largely because he hoped that he might function as his own producer. That, of course, was the kind of ambition his father could understand and, obviously, it coincided with his own career interests—such as they were—at the time. It is a minor misfortune that the younger man was not then, in the opinion of the moguls, "bankable" in the kind of films he and his father wanted to make, and that Douglas, Sr. was not capable of being the persistent producer he had once been.

Happily, however, young Fairbanks was able to manage a comeback on his own, starting with his first swashbuckler, *The Prisoner of Zenda*, in 1937, continuing through a series of light romances, and culminating in *Gunga Din* just before his father's death and *The Corsican Brothers* not long after it.

Distinguished service in World War Two (as a naval officer,

he saw action on the Murmansk run and in the invasions of Italy and the South of France) interrupted his career, and one might well say that it never recovered from that hiatus. Yet, it is interesting to contrast the son's later life with that of his father's. Although he continues to act occasionally, Fairbanks, Jr. has devoted much time to good works—and not those of a merely ceremonial sort—since the pre-war period when, as an Anglophile, he was intensely involved with the William Allen White Committee, which was strongly opposed to the America Firsters, and served as an informal Presidential envoy and fact-finder, especially among his British friends. After the war he became a successful international entrepreneur and was one of the founders of CARE. Not an idealogue—an establishment figure really—he evidently discovered a way to lead a busy, useful, and apparently fulfilling life away from fame's brightest glare. Obviously, he learned something from his father's experience. Like him, he refused to abuse the welcome he had won as an actor, refused the temptation to be outrageous. Unlike him, but perhaps because of his example, he made a graceful transition to the role of, if not quite elder statesman, then of valuable and self-esteeming world citizen.

Other than his improved relationship with his son, however, the elder Fairbanks' last two or three years were rather pathetic. He began to fail physically, his old circulatory troubles visibly afflicting him. According to some sources, the one-time tee-totaler began to drink heavily, and spend much time by himself. He did have a few contacts with younger members of the film colony; Fred Astaire remembers riding around with him of an evening in a police car, responding to radio calls. He was particularly pleased when Jayar asked him to be best man at his second marriage—to Mary Lee Epling, Huntington Hartford's first wife. But there is a sad emptiness to the end of his life, a sense of isolation from the community he had once dominated, from the entire world he once so easily bestrode.

Then, on a Saturday in early December, 1939, he attended the USC–UCLA football game and returned to the beach house in good spirits. The next morning he seemed "nervous," according to an associate, and the following day he complained of pains in his chest and left arm. Doctors were summoned, and told him he had suffered a mild heart attack. Bed rest and nursing care were ordered. If anything happened, he told his brother to tell Mary "by the clock." He also told him he was less afraid of death than he was of being an invalid.

That evening he awakened and asked the male nurse stationed at the door to open his window so he could hear the sea. He asked him how he felt and Fairbanks flashed his famous grin. "I've never felt better," he said, and a few minutes later returned to sleep. The nurse returned to his post, was just noting the time—12:45 A.M.—on his patient's chart, when he heard a deep growl from Polo, Doug's mastiff, who had remained in the bedroom with his master. The nurse looked in again and discovered that Fairbanks had died as he had lived—mercurially.

XVI

There were, of course, the usual formal, hollow tributes from the leaders of the industry. Mrs. Fred Astaire, Darryl Zanuck, Kay

Francis, and Norma Shearer, among others, called at the house. Charlie Chaplin, Joe Schenck, and Sid Grauman, the theater owner, were among the pallbearers, as were such cronies as Chuck Lewis and Geraghty. Mary Pickford was in Chicago with Buddy Rogers whom she had married in 1937, and she issued a statement saying that other obligations would prevent her from attending the funeral. "I am sure it will prove a consolation to us all to recall the joy and the glorious spirit of adventure he gave to the world. He has passed from our mortal life quickly and spontaneously as he did everything in life, but it is impossible to believe that that vibrant and gay spirit could ever perish."

She sent flowers to the "Wee Kirk O' the Heather" at Forest Lawn where the last rites were performed. Music was provided by Chico De Verdi and a four-piece ensemble which played pieces of the kind used to provide inspiration on the set of silent pictures—"La Paloma," "Cielito Lindo," that sort of thing. Sylvia's sobs could be heard rising above the words of the Episcopal burial service. Tom Mix wore his black cowboy suit.

Not long before, F. Scott Fitzgerald, whose comedown from the celebrity life had been more sudden and painful than Fairbanks', had written that the trouble was that there were no last acts in American life. Even before that, in the mid-Twenties, when there appeared to be no clouds on the horizon, the perceptive Allene Talmey had applied almost the same phrase to Fairbanks: "There are no third acts for him."

It is strange. There ought to be some more satisfactory final act to the celebrity drama than this one—the groping, stumbling exit from the stage. After all, in an unheroic age they are the only heroes we have. And in the past the heroic drama—the monomyth, as Joseph Campbell has masterfully described it—traditionally consisted of three very well-defined acts. In the first there is the drama of separation or departure; in the next comes a series of initiatory trials, leading toward a victory of sorts; the climax is a triumphant return and reintegration with society. Why is it that we deny celebrities their third-act victories? Why do so many of them seem to deny themselves that satisfaction—even when the rest of us might be content to let them enjoy it in peace?

It may be that what we have here is simply a form of rude, democratic justice. We certainly do tend to over-reward some people for minor, even accidental, achievements, while ignoring—as the liberal-minded tiresomely point out—the true pillars of the society: schoolteachers and nurses and all the rest of the people who make it function day by day. Doubtless, both the public and recipients of its adulation feel some degree of guilt over the excess that inheres in their relationship. Perhaps having loved not wisely but well, the public compensates, when it turns away from an idol, by doing so too emphatically, too cruelly. Perhaps—as seems possible in the case of Fairbanks—something in the celebrity himself unconsciously conspires with the audience to encourage a punishing dénouement for his life drama, a redress for the inexplicable and unearned good fortune he has previously enjoyed.

Perhaps everyone, in some secret corner of his mind, understands that the celebrity is only a psuedo-hero, that such figures, unlike the immortal heroes of myth, creatures of the collective unconscious, progenitors of great art, are not entitled to third acts in which the theme is reunion and reintegration. Being from the start false gods, graven images, they may inevitably be cast out into darkness, and perhaps the life of a Fairbanks—with its

desperate insistence on eternal youth, both physical and emotional
—is to be interpreted as a despairing struggle against an end that is,
again unconsciously, already known to the actor.

But here we have entered upon the darker realms of
speculation. Best to turn aside and return to the surface of our
society. If a movie star is only a psuedo-hero, who then qualifies in
the modern world—that is to say, the Global Village—as a real
hero? Do we, looking around us, see any lives which approach the
mythic levels of heroism, which we can imagine as fit subjects for
bards instead of press agents?

To ask the question is to answer it. It is absurd. We have
reached a point where it is impossible to tell the true hero (or
prophet) from the false. The media treats them all the same, mixes
them indiscriminately on its talk shows, its front pages, encourages
the writing of *romans à clef* (and scenarios *à clef* and plays *à clef*)
about them. Novelists and painters virtually cease to create works,
so busy are they creating and re-creating themselves in public.
Politicians fret about their images, complain like so many movie
stars when they get a bad—that is to say, an unmanipulated—press.
From Fairbanks dodging the photographers in a London train
station to Richard Nixon forted up inside the White House is
actually but a short and unimportant historical journey. The
distance from the youthful Fairbanks, his train of beautiful people
arranged around him at Pickfair or on some sunswept holiday, to
the Kennedy White House is, it might be added, similarly short.

We even endure, now, media-encouraged—and frightful—parodies of celebrity. One speaks here not merely of giftless
freaks—the Andy Warhols and Tiny Tims who make such good
copy, such interesting TV spots. One speaks as well of genuinely
gifted artists. Of Marlon Brando, for example. Norman Mailer has

pointed out that the "real thrill" of *Last Tango in Paris* derived from "the peephole Brando offers us on Brando." The film was shrewdly structured (or rather restructured by its director, Bernardo Bertolucci, after Brando committed to it) so that, first of all, it completed the circle of Brando's public career. (His character is, in effect, a combination of his most famous youthful parts—Stanley Kowalski in *Streetcar*, the rebellious gang leader of *The Wild One*, Terry Mulloy of *On the Waterfront*—glimpsed twenty to twenty-five years later as he passes melodramatically through the midlife crisis.) The film does satisfy our "whatever became of . . . ?" "where are they now?" curiosity about those people, who were, though fictions, so indelibly a part of a generation's sensibility that they had lives outside their original fictional frames.

More important, by encouraging Brando to improvise as freely as he could—to use as many of his own memories and associations and preoccupations to give this character depth and dimension—Bertolucci encouraged a quantum leap in the celebrity game. All actors have always given us something of themselves in performance. But their sexual fantasies? Their free associations? The sound of their inner voices, the streams of consciousness unmediated? Never. Or, as Mailer says: "Pandemonium of pleasure in the house. . . . The crowd's joy is that a national celebrity is being obscene on screen. To measure the media magnetism of such an act, ask yourself how many hundreds of miles you might drive to hear Richard Nixon speak a line like: 'We're just taking a flying fuck at a rolling doughnut.' . . .

"Let us recognize the phenomenon. It would be so surrealistic an act, we could not pass Nixon by. Surrealism has become our objective correlative. A private glimpse of the great becomes the alchemy of the media, the fool's gold of the century of communication. In the age of television we know everything about the great but how they fart—the ass wind is, ergo, our trade wind."

So, as Brando realized, and Mailer, watching, recognized, we had here a peculiar act of genius, one that faltered only when it failed to cross the final barrier and reveal to us how a celebrity really has intercourse—not merely miming the act, as Brando did. It can only be a matter of time before some major star offers us this revelation; already the screens of the X-rated theaters are filled with young women rather pathetically reversing this process—hoping that by revealing how they have intercourse, they will become stars. (One is, indeed, unreasonably titillated by the revelation that the young mother of the Ivory Snow commercials is appearing in a dirty movie.)

But of course the parodies of the celebrity system do not stop with show biz. Far from it. Similar and more monstrous reversals now occur in areas we were not long ago pleased to regard as safely insulated from such actor-like goings-on. One thinks, of course, of the nonideological youthful "revolutionaries" of a few years ago, who found in violence, and threats of violence, a shortcut to notoriety. One thinks also of the Abbie Hoffmans and the Jerry Rubins who achieved a degree of temporary political importance through the simple act of achieving personal notoriety—a reversal of the customary chain of events in this realm of endeavor. One thinks, too, of the outright psychopaths who have found—in political assassination or, say, in the hijacking of airliners—an extremely tempting shortcut to the essence of celebrity, which is the ability to impose themselves on the consciousness of strangers, without any of the struggle and self-discipline that, for instance, even the most beautiful starlet must undergo. To be sure, they must be prepared to sacrifice their freedom—if not their very lives—to achieve their fame, but have we not been fed for generations on the knowledge that the celebrity sacrifices much freedom, and not occasionally many years of his life, to that end? Indeed, isn't that one of the themes of Fairbanks' life? To be sure, these parody celebrities achieve little wealth—except what can be realized on their autobiographies, most of which goes for attorneys' fees, but have we not learned that in the upper brackets you don't get to keep much, anyway? And, besides, don't we understand from the stars themselves that wealth is, in their cases, a by-product, not the true end of their existences? "It's lonely at the top," Arthur Bremer, would-be murderer of George Wallace, murmurs, and the hidden link between the envied top and the envious bottom of society becomes clear. And turns into a bridge that can be crossed by the murderously daring.

We cannot all be wealthy or beautiful or gifted—that constant of existence remains unchanged by the last half century. But it is now clear that one of the rewards of those conditions—celebrity—is available to all. Democratically. On the cheap. The question of authenticity now endlessly recurs. For everyone is now what very few were only a little while ago—an actor. Politicians and presumptive saints, artists and critics, athletes and murderers—all are now actors. And we are fascinated, almost pornographically, by their gestures and asides, peering intently at their images as they bombard us, seeking in them clues as to who among them bears true witness to our times, who false. Finally, it seems, we destroy celebrity—and encourage the celebrity's impulses to self-destruction—as a radical attempt to clarify the confusion between private self and public self, which may also be read as a confusion between ends and means, between reality and metaphor. The destruction only *seems* casual or inexplicable. Actually, it is very nearly inevitable, the only hope being a final transformation from celebrity existence to existence as a living institution or sage, a transformation in our times most often accomplished by the artist.

XVII

It has been our pleasure, of late, to consider the entire movie business a has-been. That, too, is a form of compensatory punishment (and self-punishment). We allowed ourselves to care too much about it, to let it and its people and its legends mean too much to us, fill too many of the empty spaces in our time and minds. And when the basic game it invented—and it was that game, not the art which was occasionally its by-product, that fascinated us—was taken over, expanded into all the other significant areas of public life, we permitted ourselves the luxury of contempt, the delusion that "the industry" was impotent, dying. The studios are shuttered, empty and echoing, the new myth, the antimyth, tells us. Hollywood is a ghost town.

But it is a delusion, based on the fact that the number of feature films produced yearly has declined, that the number of them produced in the old manner, on the back lots and soundstages of the studios, has declined even more radically. That, however, is an insignificant fact. Where do we imagine they're making all those television shows that preoccupy us? And where do we imagine the decisions about packaging and financing them—and the not inconsiderable number of theatrical films still being produced—are made? Power simply wears a different face now, and some of its practices have been revised. But it abides. Joan Didion, the novelist and essayist, calls Hollywood "the last extant stable society," and she does not exaggerate very much. "At midwinter in the survivors' big houses off Benedict Canyon the fireplaces blaze all day with scrub oak and eucalyptus, the French windows are opened wide to the subtropical sun, the rooms filled with white phalaenopsis and cymbidium orchids and needlepoint rugs and the requisite scent of Rigaud candles. Dinner guests pick with vermeil forks at broiled fish and limestone lettuce *vinaigrette,* decline dessert, adjourn to the screening room and settle down . . . with a little seltzer in a Baccarat glass."

The last extant stable society. Enjoying the style Doug and Mary set for it a half century before. Enjoying it because, with one or two others, they established the necessity of the star—no, the celebrity—as central not merely to their business, but to everyone's business in this century. In particular, that was his doing. For it was he—not his wife, not his friend Chaplin, not any of the others—who cheerfully, perhaps unthinkingly, opened up his life, that rich good life, to the public, and invited them to participate in it, enjoy it with him. And it was he who then revolted against their endless intrusions, he who acted out, in the end, the archetypical career drama of the star, demonstrating that though it encompassed all the roles he played, it far transcended all of them. It was he who demonstrated—it was by far his most fabulous stunt, the more so since he never foresaw its full effects—that anyone of talent, or merely will, could play this larger, juicier role in any public walk of life.* He found the machinery of the media there, waiting for him,

---

* The novelist Harvey Swados suggested that J. D. Salinger learned his public manner from

like one of his sets, and he bounded daringly, childishly, wonderfully, about in it—a delight to the eye, an example to many, forgetting only to check his handholds, make sure there was an escape route, in the end perhaps dying because he could not find his way out.

Perhaps it is as well. Perhaps he understood the whole thing better than anyone knew, understood the correctness of an early exit. Pickford and her last juvenile live on at Pickfair and, in 1971, when they arranged a limited re-release of her early movies, a small number of journalists was permitted to penetrate the legendary pile. Butlers served champagne and hors d'oeuvres beneath the Remingtons, while Buddy Rogers, tanned and handsomely gray, manipulated a tape recorder containing an awkward speech of welcome by Mary. It ended and Rogers proclaimed eagerly, "She's a million times better than that. A million times better than that. She's been sick, you know. She was 'My Best Girl' in 1927 and she's still my best girl."

Whereupon he guided them through the rest of the mansion, pausing outside her bedroom. "Darling, all your friends are here," he cried. He opened the door and leaned inside. A few of the reporters heard a soft murmur emanating from the room. "Give them what?" Rogers asked. "Give them your love. Mary says to give you her love."

She is eighty now. She has had an operation for cataracts. She is reported to be upset by the smutty movies she understands they are producing nowadays and by those tales of the deserted studios. She never ventures forth, though by special dispensation you can sometimes speak to her on the phone. Right after lunch is a good

---

Garbo, that Hemingway was Fairbanks' literary inheritor. The game of analogs can be indefinitely extended in literature. And in other fields.

time. She tells inquirers that she reads the Bible and Shakespeare, scarcely watches the color TV Buddy gave her, looks neither at new movies nor her old ones. She says she misses Hedda Hopper. People talk about the end of an era. But what was significant about her era has not ended. Rather, it is everywhere—so much a part of our lives that we scarcely notice it any more. One sometimes envies her isolation.

ACKNOWLEDGMENTS AND BIBLIOGRAPHICAL NOTE

This book began as an article for *American Heritage*, so my first debt of gratitude is to Oliver Jensen and Barbara Klaw of that publication, who commissioned it, and to the magazine itself for permission to reprint portions of the essay here. After the piece appeared in December 1971, I was surprised and delighted to receive from Douglas Fairbanks, Jr., an extremely long letter—some twenty single-spaced pages—commenting on and criticizing the article as it appeared (it had been somewhat truncated for reasons of space). It was the receipt of that letter, containing so much information and so many insights not available in the printed sources on his father's life, that stimulated thoughts of expanding the article into a small book, so I am grateful to him, not only for permission to reprint portions of that document, but for the implicit suggestion that there was more here than first met my eye.

Around the time I was working on the Fairbanks piece for *Heritage*, I was discussing with two friends, David Bazelon and Dr. Leslie H. Farber, the possibility of collaborating on some sort of study of the celebrity system in America, and though we have yet to settle down to it, they will recognize many of their ideas in this book. I am more than pleased to recognize publicly their contributions to my thinking.

Two other coincidences also contributed to this book. In the past few years I have been working on a biography of D. W. Griffith and on some television programs dealing with American movie history. In the course of that work I have had the enormous pleasure of interviewing a number of Fairbanks' contemporaries, and his name kept coming up. I am therefore grateful to Allan Dwan, Howard Hawks, Raoul Walsh, William A. Wellman, and Bennie Zeidman for their thoughts on this subject. Finally, a word of gratitude to Michael Korda of Simon and Schuster, who is the most patient man I know. He has been forced to wait an unconscionable amount of time for the Griffith, but even so, graciously granted me permission to take time off from a contractual obligation in order to do this book.

The basic print source on my subject is *Douglas Fairbanks: The Fourth Musketeer* by Ralph Hancock and Letitia Fairbanks (Henry Holt, 1953) and it is, as these affairs go, quite an excellent biography of an actor—combining fondness for the subject with a high degree of objectivity and good research. The basic critical document is Alistair Cooke's *Douglas Fairbanks: The Making of a Screen Character* (Museum of Modern Art, 1940). I have here and there quarreled with it in these pages, but it remains one of the few distinguished studies of movie iconography. Brian Connell's *Knight Errant*, a biography of Douglas Fairbanks, Jr. (London: Hodder and Stoughton, 1955) includes much valuable material contributed by members of the family. In addition, a good deal of interest is to be found in the autobiographies of his contemporaries. To wit: *Sunshine and Shadow* by Mary Pickford (Doubleday, 1955); *Chaplin: My Autobiography* by Charles Chaplin (Simon and Schuster, 1964); *A Girl Like I* by Anita Loos (Viking, 1966); *The Honeycomb* by Adela Rogers St. John (Doubleday, 1969). There are two interesting contemporary views of Fairbanks, one an essay in *Doug and Mary and Others* by Allene Talmey (Macey-Masius, 1927), the other an article by Vachel Lindsay, "The Great Douglas Fairbanks," which appeared in *The Ladies' Home Journal* in August 1926. I am grateful to George Pratt of Eastman House for calling the latter to my attention. Mr. Pratt is also the editor of a distinguished and carefully annotated anthology of contemporary writing about the silent screen, *Spellbound in Darkness*, a multilith publication of the University of Rochester, which by the time this book appears is scheduled to be published in a more readily available form by a commercial publisher. Similarly useful is *American Film Criticism from the Beginnings to Citizen Kane*, edited by Stanley Kauffmann with Bruce Henstell (Liveright, 1972) and *Film Notes*, a collection of program notes edited by Eileen Bowser and published in 1969 by the Museum of Modern Art, for which they were originally written. Also to be mentioned as a general source of information and delight is Edward Wagenknecht's reminiscences of movie-going in his youth, *Movies in the Age of Innocence* (University of Oklahoma Press, 1962), while Alexander Walker's *Stardom* (Stein and Day, 1970) is the most detailed and critically interesting study of movie stardom as an institution. On the more general matter of the celebrity system I found Daniel J. Boorstin's *The Image: or What Happened to the American Dream* (Atheneum, 1962) and C. Wright Mills's *The Power Elite* (Oxford University Press, 1956) most helpful. I also relied heavily on Norman Mailer's "A Transit to Narcissus," *The New York Review of Books*, May 17, 1973, and on Joseph L. Mankiewicz's remarks about the problem of marriage in the celebrity world. His insights are unique and they are to be found in his colloquy with Gary Carey, which stands as the introduction to the recent republication of his most memorable screenplay in a book called *More About All About Eve* (Random House, 1972). Finally, it is a pleasure to acknowledge Aljean Harmetz's article, in the *New York Times*, March 28, 1971, which is the major source of my information about life at Pickfair now. In addition, of course, this study owes much to the ephemeral journalism, yellow and crumbling, which is to be found in a couple of magazine morgues to which, happily, I had access.

As always, I am grateful to my wife, Jill, for her patience, wit, and encouragement—and, in this case, for her assistance on picture research—and to my friend and editor Richard Kluger for his discreet editorial pencil and, more than that, for being one of the rare people in publishing who require no more than one explanation of what you think you're doing.

RICHARD SCHICKEL
April 5, 1973

INDEX

ABOUT THE AUTHOR

Richard Schickel was the movie critic for *Life* magazine until it ceased publication in 1972. He is now a reviewer for *Time*. Among his previous books are *Second Sight: Notes on Some Movies, 1965–70*; *The Disney Version*; *Movies: The History of an Art and an Institution*; *The Stars*; *The World of Carnegie Hall*; and a story for children, *The Gentle Knight*. He wrote the Public Broadcasting System television specials *The Movie Crazy Years* and *Hollywood: You Must Remember This*, and he has just written, directed, and produced the PBS series *The Men Who Made the Movies*. He is married to Julia Whedon, the writer, and they live in Manhattan. They have two children, Erika and Jessica.